A *publication of the*
75th Anniversary of The University of Chicago

ROCKEFELLER
CHAPEL
SERMONS

ROCKEFELLER CHAPEL SERMONS

Of Recent Years

Compiled by
DONOVAN E. SMUCKER

THE UNIVERSITY OF CHICAGO PRESS
Chicago and London

Library of Congress Catalog Card Number: 66-30215

THE UNIVERSITY OF CHICAGO PRESS, CHICAGO & LONDON
The University of Toronto Press, Toronto 5, Canada

© *1967 by The University of Chicago*
Published 1967
Printed in the United States of America

Foreword

Preaching in the latter half of the twentieth century is a precarious business. It is widely acknowledged that the art of preaching, which was Protestantism's great contribution to the religious life of the world, has fallen to a low place in the hierarchy of significant forms of human communication. It remains to be seen whether recent efforts, among Protestants and Roman Catholics alike, to recover a more significant place for the sermon within the structure of public worship will alter the present trend.

Preaching has lost much of its power, in part at least because words have become cheap in our time. Hawkers of every conceivable cause and product in our acquisitive society have bombarded our ears with their exaggerated claims and half-truths, until sensitive men and women can only turn away in deliberate deafness. Even our children learn early to discount the blabber of the radio and television commercial—but at the high cost of never knowing when the truth is being spoken.

No longer are words reliable indicators of the truth of a situation. Our age has prostituted information into propaganda; it has substituted defensive rationalizations for reason, and it has hired words and slogans to shield acts of deceit, treachery, and even war. The ancient breach between profession and performance is still with us, tempting us to the simple generalization that people are to be trusted only on the basis of their

692.66

actions. What this cliché too easily forgets is that whenever *doing* is disengaged from verbal interpretation, it becomes unintelligible and meaningless. Speaking, on the other hand, which bears no viable and authentic relation to *doing* and *being*, is nonsense. It may be that a lack of vitality and relevance has vitiated the power of contemporary preaching more than anything else. In any case, the problem is acute and will not be solved by any ready-made gimmicks or forensic novelties.

Sermons are preached weekly in tens of thousands of pulpits across the country, and yet it is problematic how decisive they are in shaping either the direction of our personal living or the substance of our common life. Those of us who are foolish enough to contend that preaching can still be a viable instrument for exploring the issues of existential importance for modern man find ourselves in a decreasing minority among the ordained clergy of America. Students in theological seminaries are fascinated by all manner of exotic and specialized ministries, but only a handful are admittedly excited by the prospects of the preaching ministry.

The reader of these sermons will do well to employ his imagination in reconstructing the setting and the atmosphere in which they were delivered if he would enjoy a measure of their power and liveliness. A sermon, after all, is not primarily a form of writing but of human discourse involving the presence and personality of the preacher and the responsive listening of a congregation. Interesting essays may be written for the instruction and edification of people generally in which the only encounter of persons is through the media of pen, ink, and paper, but a sermon is different. It remains that peculiar form of speaking which depends in largest measure upon the living context in which it is being delivered for its deepest appreciation and effectiveness as an instrument of human communication.

These sermons constitute an earnest attempt by a vast company of men to clarify, deepen, and inspire the lives of those who are willing to expose themselves to this "not-so-highly-regarded" endeavor. Those who have come to preach in the chapel through the years have spoken from that boundary situation which marks the sometimes painful and sometimes glorious point where the temporal and the eternal meet and where men speak to other men conscious of the mystery and power which circumscribes their lives. With St. Paul they try to remember that they "have this treasure in earthen vessels to show that the transcendent power belongs to God" and not to them. Christians preach with confidence not in their cleverness but rather in the transforming power of a word which they dare to believe is not irrelevant to the nature and destiny of all mankind.

E. Spencer Parsons, *Dean*

Rockefeller Memorial Chapel
University of Chicago

Acknowledgments

The editor and publishers wish to thank the following for their permission to use material in this book:

"The Brothers" by B. Davie Napier. Copyright 1966. Reprinted by permission of Fortress Press.

"The Appearances of Our Risen Lord" by W. B. Blakemore. From *Encountering God*, by permission of The Bethany Press.

"The Good I Will, I Do Not" by Paul Tillich. Printed by permission of Robert C. Kimball, Literary Executor for the estate of Paul Tillich.

"The Word of the God Who Won't Talk" by Tom F. Driver. Printed by permission of the author.

Introduction

At the corner of Woodlawn and Fifty-ninth Street, just off the Midway, on the University of Chicago campus, stands the Rockefeller Memorial Chapel. It was built and endowed by the family whose benefactions launched the institution seventy-five years ago. Dedicated in 1928, it constrasts with King's College Chapel, Cambridge, the cornerstone of which was laid in 1446. The magnificence of the Chicago structure places it on any list of great university chapels, ancient or modern, such as those at Princeton, Duke, Cambridge, and Oxford. Whatever the acids of modernity have done to these universities, the chapels symbolize the present reality of their religious origins.

Rockefeller Chapel fulfills many roles. It is the Cathedral of the Midwest, a building which has a central location, massive size, and Gothic grandeur unique in this region of America. As such it is a tourist sight, a place to see or in which to attend a service during a visit to Chicago.

In contrast to the dominant modern mood of all our art forms, the architecture of the building is a permanent tribute to the Gothic genius for infinity expressed through the pointed arch, high roofs, and lancet windows. The probability of erecting a similar church elsewhere is unlikely, since most recent religious buildings suggest that modern design is the norm in this era and perhaps will be in those to come.

Along with its primary function as a center of worship, the chapel provides a majestic setting for the highest mo-

ments of academic ritual. Everyone who has received an under-
graduate or advanced degree at Chicago since 1928 has heard
the joyous sound of the carillon calling the successful students to
the convocation. In the vastness of the chapel the long center
aisle is a perfect place for the procession of costumed scholars
reminding everyone present of the origins of the universities in
the Middle Ages and dramatizing the training of the faculty in
the leading institutions of the Western world. The chapel has
also bestowed its graces of the spirit on occasions of recognition
for Prime Minister Nehru, Albert Schweitzer, Karl Barth, and
other distinguished leaders whose presence called for a special
celebration.

The love of the dramatic sometimes overwhelms the
tendency to doubt and debunk. Recently the University of Chicago redesigned the black academic robe and austere mortar
board. Now the gown is maroon, topped off with a soft bonnet in
the Oxbridge pattern. Marburg, Madrid, Harvard, and Paris no
longer monopolize color in the Rockefeller convocations. At last
costume has come to terms with tradition—even though the
modern man wearing the new colors may be an expert in econo-
metrics or molecular biology.

Yet, the convocations remain secondary to the major
role of the chapel as a center for Christian services. This book
focuses on the spoken word in that ministry. The volume will
create a false impression if it implies that the chapel is only a
preaching station. The worship service has moved from an eclec-
tic pattern to an impressive catholicity of Protestant orientation.
Under Richard Vikstrom the organ and choir have reached
heights seldom attained in a university chapel. The carillon
carries this same ministry to that largest of all congregations in
any academic community—the "outsiders" who are unwilling to
come to a formal worship service.

Professor Sittler declared in one of his sermons that
the university pulpit stands halfway between the committed faith
that placed her there and the disinterested inquiry that surrounds
her. He continued by noting that the university chapel is not a
church related to a particular religious community, an explicit
witnessing and confessing congregation. But he insisted on the

advantages of preaching in a chapel in this setting, the desire of his hearers for clarity, depth, and precision of thought. "It is the truth that counts," Professor Sittler said, "and if the faith cannot be commended as guaranteeing a lubricant for scratchy life, or a glue to hold together a threatened republic (both contemporary aberrations!) that is nothing against the truth."

There are college and university chapels which offer regular or associate membership to students. At Lafayette College the chapel is a congregation organized under the polity of the Presbyterian church with ruling elders, a Session, and a membership roll. Chicago has never functioned with this pattern. It has no regular membership even though there may be a hard core of people in the community who regularly attend despite the constant flux characteristic of academic neighborhoods. Even if Hyde Park and its university were stable societies, the chapel would still choose the present pattern as appropriate in a world marked by Christian diversity and pluralism.

Panofsky may be correct in linking the origins of Gothic architecture to scholastic philosophy. In any case the deans of Rockefeller Chapel have never accepted this ancient marriage for the twentieth century. From the very beginning of his leadership, Charles W. Gilkey invited many speakers who were neither scholastics nor clergymen. In this group were W. E. B. Du Bois, James Weldon Johnson, Frances Perkins, Jane Addams, Mary E. Woolley, Robert Redfield, Arthur H. Compton, Max Otto, Pierre van Paassen, Harry Overstreet, Frank Graham, Robert Maynard Hutchins, and Norman Thomas, the latter speaking seven times between 1931 and 1939. Lest the reader think that the clergy were overlooked, it is important to note that Dean Gilkey selected ministers as varied in outlook as John Haynes Holmes, Robert E. Speer, Harry Emerson Fosdick, Ernest Fremont Tittle, George A. Buttrick, and Canon V. A. Demant. If this was a bewildering pattern it was also exciting.

Then as now the chapel struck a balance between continuity of preaching by the resident staff and variety introduced by speakers from other places. Indeed, Dean Gilkey, who preached 180 sermons in the chapel, fixed the pattern of audacious discourse in the setting of a worship service marked by dignity and beauty. His successor, John Beauchamp Thompson, combined social concern with literary imagination, plunging into political controversy with the aplomb of Rauschenbusch or William Temple. Under the leadership of W. Barnett Blakemore the worship service began to reflect a Protestant catholicity which went beyond the resources of liberal Protestantism, and his preaching was based on a profound use of modern biblical scholarship. The speakers he invited, however, were less varied than those of the earlier periods.

Among the more frequent visitors in recent years Joseph Sittler revealed a poetic diction which reclothed the Christian faith in modern speech as lyrical as the Bible of Luther or King James. He was also a representative figure among the many Lutherans who brought a new dimension of faith to the Divinity School, the chapel, and the university as a whole. The present dean, E. Spencer Parsons, began his ministry in the autumn quarter of 1965 by continuing the precedent set by Dr. Gilkey in coming from nearby Hyde Park Baptist Church.

Looking over the nearly forty years of the chapel under a gifted staff, one is not hard pressed to name the visiting ministers with the greatest impact: Harry Emerson Fosdick, Reinhold Niebuhr, and Paul Tillich. In different ways the sermons of these three men were real occasions in the university. Dr. Fosdick carried the mystique of a major figure in the fundamentalist-modernist controversy. He combined piercing clarity with memorable illustrations while mounting to climaxes of controlled emotional intensity. Although he sought to rid the Christain faith of false accretions, his central thrust was an affirmation of hope. Reinhold Niebuhr punctured illusions—liberal, orthodox, and humanist—with analytical power sparkling with paradox and irony. In the pulpit Paul Tillich transformed his ponderous, sometimes obscure theology into a luminous restatement of the Christian faith for the twentieth century. He spoke as one having authority, the authority of experience with all he was describing. His sermons had a deep sobriety touched with an amazing humility. The last sermon Paul Tillich preached in Rockefeller Chapel was presented on April 25, 1965, at the beginning of the university Festival of the Arts. Significantly, it was a message of hope, with a final section devoted to his view of death and the Eternal. It is a profound tribute to the power of preaching that these three giants of the pulpit could speak with such effectiveness in a great university. The eleven appearances of Tillich (1949–65), the dozen messages of Fosdick (1929–50) and the twenty-five sermons of Niebuhr (1930–51) will never be forgotten. Indeed, it is correct to say that their theological insights were expressed most clearly and most powerfully in the idiom of preaching.

It is a matter of regret that the sermons of Niebuhr and Fosdick were not available for this volume. Selections were restricted to the years beginning in 1960 because Dean Blakemore made the important decision in that year to tape, transcribe, and duplicate the addresses. Before then, the preachers were not expected to leave their manuscripts or notes with the chapel staff. What a feast it would have been to have not only Niebuhr and Fosdick but Jane Addams, W. E. B. Du Bois, and—in 1959—Martin Luther King. On the other hand, nearly one hundred men have had their addresses recorded since 1960; and a dozen of these individuals made frequent Sunday appearances. The decision was made to select the best from the list of several hundred sermons available. Excellence was the criterion rather than the name and background of the speaker.

This book reveals that university sermons are not qualitatively different from those presented away from an academic community. Perhaps there is greater audacity in grappling with rugged questions, greater freedom of utterance, more allusions to the artistic media, and generally less conventional ways of thought. These, however, are only differences of degree, since college people have the same fears, dilemmas, and hopes as any other group of people in our time. Proof of this is the long and successful tradition of broadcasting the services· over Chicago radio station WGN. In connection with that ministry the greatest response ever given to any one sermon was that given to "The Christian and Grief" by Granger E. Westberg, formerly Associate Professor of Religion and Health in both the medical and theological faculties of the university. Next to this sermon the highest response was accorded the presentations of Paul Tillich.

The sermons in the chapel tend to be topical in nature, often discussing a particular problem having no direct relationship to the Bible, as in the case of Sidney Mead's "The Lost Dimension and the Age of Longing." This presents an analysis of a religious situation in which the speaker is personally involved: hence it is a sermon and not a lecture.

Yet the Bible is frequently and directly used as the foundation for chapel sermons. Indeed, the professor of preaching at Princeton commended Dean Blakemore for his use of the Scriptures in the face of everything critical scholarship has done. The first sermons of Dean Parsons suggest he possesses the same gift. Moreover, the messages of the two Jewish preachers in this book reveal that biblical categories are very much alive in contemporary Judaism. All in all, these sermons confirm the survival of the Bible after a microscopic and at times ruthless examination.

This collection also reveals the possibility of a solidly theological approach. Indeed a presentation undergirded with real theological insight is always to be preferred to the patchwork structure displayed by topical sermons. There is no evidence that serious theological concern is irrelevant or unedifying: the great congregations which assembled for Niebuhr and Tillich are clearly cases in point.

Perhaps the most striking difference between the sixties and the earlier decades of the chapel is a less frontal and less frequent attack on social questions. The concern is there but is chastened by the more realistic mood of the postwar years, a greater awareness of complexity, and a sense of the volatility of local issues. A good example of the new social prophet in the pulpit is Gibson Winter, Professor of Ethics and Society in the Divinity School. Professor Winter speaks with special awareness of the tough complexities of the race problem, north and south. Like an Old Testament prophet, he locates the demon of privatism, the retreat into a personal salvation denying the corporate reality of man's existence; then he relates this to a conflict of cosmic proportions drawn from a New Testament text.

It is understandable that a common core of conviction will be difficult to find in a chapel where Jewish rabbis join Anglican, Orthodox, Lutheran, Reformed, free Protestant, and

—before long—Roman Catholic preachers, and where speakers from overseas have included visitors from the worlds of Shintoism, Hinduism, Islam, and Coptic Christianity. Nevertheless, there is continuity and even some unity, as the chapel of the university reflects the multiversity in her midst.

The University of Chicago has always been sensitive to new theological trends. In this book several of these are mirrored and confronted—the fundamental issue of the existence of God, the crisis in religious language, the diversity of religious claims, and the loss of authority. The approaches vary from William Graham Cole's easy conversational tone in his sermon "G—O—D" to Kyle Haselden's ringing reaffirmation of Christ's lordship in "The Lights and the Light."

The editor expresses his gratitude for the assistance of Dean Blakemore, Dean Parsons, and Miss Jane Hardy of the chapel staff. To the many individuals whose sermons had to be excluded due to lack of space he expresses his sincere regrets.

The book is sent forth on the seventy-fifth anniversary of the university with the editor's personal delight in being counted among its alumni.

Donovan E. Smucker

Contents

4   THE PROPHETIC CALL

5   GRIEF, DEATH, AND
THE ETERNAL

6   OTHER FAITHS, OTHER LANDS

1

UNIVERSITY: CHAPEL, STUDENTS, AND COMMUNITY

Effort and Serenity

By Joseph Sittler
The University of Chicago

This foundation exists and is maintained for the worship of God. This chapel and all that takes place in it are not mere ceremonial. Ceremonial often exists; and it often takes the form of a chapel on a college or a university campus—a kind of a vague benediction that the university or the college waves in the general direction of a tradition which is acknowledged to be dead, but it makes good public relations to act as if it weren't. A ceremony has been described as an outward sign of a vitality that once had force and meaning, but whose demise is now nostalgically remembered with appropriate actions and noises which continue the sheer momentum of the tradition—like changing the guard at Buckingham Palace. This chapel is not ceremonial. The university's chapel is not understood as a bastion of moral admonition, a sort of religious maiden aunt who flutters around the outer ethical edges of the behavioral sciences. Nor is the chapel to be understood as an adjunct of the office of the dean of students, disengaged, that is, from the life of the university, but retained in order to soften the hard-nosed public image of a tough-minded faculty and to ameliorate the more dramatic forms of student indiscretion.

This chapel actually exists, and there are services of the worship of God here, because there really exists in history a peculiar community. This peculiar community exists as affirming and acknowledging that there *is* a God, that something of His

3

nature is knowable and has been disclosed, that He has a will
and a purpose and exercises redemptive force in history, and that
something of this can be known and obeyed. This peculiar community is a historical datum of enormous complexity, variety,
scope, and creativity. It has shaped entire cultures; it has in-
formed whole ways of beholding and dealing with the world; it
has proposed to man's reflection massive intellectual systems,
and it has penetrated mind and disposition and human purpose
with specifiable and energetic force. Now this activity, this history, these affirmations peculiar to this community are a proper
enquiry for university attention, and this free university includes
such within the company of studies which it thinks appropriate
to a university. I asked that there be read this morning from the
lectern the two lessons—one from the Old and one from the
New Testament. First, the Twenty-fifth Psalm, a song through
one man of a whole people beset by trouble, but willing in
trouble to trust, and as a function of that trusting to "wait on
the Lord" and have faith. And, second, the great New Testament
lesson, its serenity and sobriety—"Be not anxious"—forged not
out of kind of detached and non-actual piety, but out of the tears
and the fears of life. These lessons were chosen as a kind of traditional proposal of a possibility. They are like a background of
promise against which I want to ask a question.

If each of us were to ask of himself or of one of his
fellows what it is that he most desires in life, he would find the
answer hard to come by. For ultimate desire is steady and volatile
stuff; it continues to bubble unceasingly within every vessel of
concrete purpose and intention which we dream up to enclose it.
It always seems to continue bubbling when the enclosures for
the fulfillment of desire have a seeming adequacy. When a man
is able to state what it is that he really desires and begins to make
a sentence about it, he knows while the sentence is forming that
he is not saying what it is he most profoundly desires. He knows
that concrete purposes are always penultimate, that the full
reality of man's desire is both illusive, steady, relentless, and
unnamable.

A university is a product of this volatile desire in life,
and it orders its work along paths always changing and always

freshly rich with the good and the promising and the necessary that seem right to do in virtue of things that men desire. Several illustrations: men's desire to know. The university is committed to knowledge, to gain and verify it, to increase the sum of it, to transmit it, to honor it against all unknowing and uncaring, and to have delight in it. Men desire order, not only outward order, but the way of mind and sensibility whereby one might comprehend what tends toward order. Not only outward order, but to learn to distinguish the better from the worse, the central and the steady from the peripheral and the passing, and by life concerned about things as they have been and are, learn perhaps to cast some light upon novel and ever-emerging forms of disorder. Men desire justice. A university serves this desire, not by enactments which are more just than those that currently prevail, but by the excision and the laying bare of the anatomy and the etiology of injustice, socially, economically, and every other way. A university is always an effort to find the meaning of justice, remembering that justice is a vision before it is a matter of law, that justice is always the effort to see men clearly, of understanding men's needs, desires, and potentialities in privacy and in their multiple relationships in the world. In the Old Testament, righteousness, truth, goodness, and justice are all aspects of a single conception. Righteous means "right"-ness; justice means something very close to having things "right," and in this chapel throughout the year is added this Old Testament voice of "righteousness" to the symphony of university study.

All these things are related to what men ultimately desire, but none of them alone adds up to, nor do all of them together constitute or secure, the quieting of what it is that men ultimately desire. We live, and work, and feel, and think relentlessly forward to desires which transcend all conceptual statements of what they are and actual achievements of what we have believed them to be possible to be quieted by. In the history of our culture there have been efforts to specify by name what it is that men most desire of themselves or of their world. There are several illustrations that might be useful. In Hellas the name for that man to whom all men looked as the man in whom desires are quieted was the *megalopsychos*—"the large-minded man," the man in whom there was no eccentricity or forgotten idiosyncrasy, the man as rightly proportioned as the entablature of the temple—every detail wrought out and in just proportion.

The Renaissance created a kind of model of the man who fulfils his desires. He was the magnanimous man. One can get the image of him in *Castiglioni* or in Erasmus' *Letters to a Christian Prince*. He was to be a man who was at home in all worlds, in the world of politics, in the immediate world of civil affairs, a man who was adept at warfare and in the arts of peace, a man who knew how to dispose all things with justice, right use, and good taste—the magnanimous man.

Israel never stated the problem that way. Israel never assumed that the self could realize selfhood or its desire by a maturation or a reproportioning of the given vitalities *of* the self, *from* the self, *for* the self, or for the self among other selves. The self as Israel confesses it in this Twenty-fifth Psalm, is always a self in a *world whose own selfhood* is a creature of a creator. And the Twenty-fifth Psalm is simply incomprehensible apart from that assumption at the beginning. Let me point out two words in the Psalm. The Psalm says, "To Thee, O Lord, I lift up my soul, Oh my Lord, I trust in Thee." It goes immediately from this word about trust to the word that caused me to want to speak about it and to remind you of it on this particular day, because the third verse says, "For Thee I wait all the day long." I wait! Now, to wait in the Lord does not seem a very exciting way to live. There seems to be something almost gauche about introducing this old world of waiting into what noises you have heard made at you this week and you will hear more next week about what is required—the exactness of study and preparation, "get with it," "get going," and "these are the ways to do it." Then you come to the chapel and a man preaches about waiting! It seems a very reckless, unattractive image to thrust into the properly carbonated feelings which you bring to this experience this week. But the strange thing about the way the word "wait" works in this Psalm is that the word is the most active word in the Psalm and by no means an invitation to total collapse. The way the word works in the Psalm is this: to wait upon that in which one trusts is to be fiercely active in the midst of the lives which the Psalmist affirms is supported and presided over by the one in whom he trusts. Waiting is not a collapse; it is His program. Not an empty stillness, but a kind of resolution in trust, at the heart of which there is a stillness not of my making, not of my destroying—although it is of my betraying.

And I submit this word as an appropriate word as we enter a new term in this university on the ground of two final points, repeating here what I was able to say about a month ago at the time students at the other end of process were leaving this university. But I think that what I said then about the nature of this moment in university study, as that is placed contrapuntally over against what the Psalm says, "to wait," is right to say now.

A university claims to liberate the mind, and when liberal, that is, liberating, studies are properly done, they achieve that. We are liberated from loneliness by accepting membership in a larger company, a longer time, a richer conversation in thought and action. We are indeed liberated from stifling egocentricity, for our hot little selfhood *is* questioned, challenged, bewildered. And if we stay with it, supported by what an English teacher in Cambridge once called "residency among all that saddens, gladdens, maddens us men and women in this brief and beautiful traject which yet must be home for a while, the anchorage of our hearts," we have a chance to achieve a real liberation.

But this liberation is ultimately a liberation into the most problematic of all positions. The brighter we are, the more quickly this is liable to dawn upon us. And if we avoid the stupefactions of a seductive culture, this liberation into life's unsystematic, this most problematic of all liberations, this conviction that that's the way things are, is liable to be permanent. Now, to be sure, we make penultimate decisions and resolutions on the way; otherwise we couldn't live. We say, "I can do this better than that. This realm of discourse is more appropriate to my endowments that that, and this shall be the operational theater of my life." And we can indeed become so involved in these penultimate answers to ultimate questions and become so seduced by the busy-ness within an operational life that we can mask the question from our attention or anesthetize our trouble within it.

Something like that seems to me to be the present position. It is not characteristic of a university student now entering to be told or invited to suppose that here is a guaranteed procedure whereby solutions to problems can be found or preparation for those sure solutions achieved. But life in a university is rather an introduction to life in the world that must get on with some task and constructions and approximations for which there are no guaranteed solutions—and the university lies in its teeth if it assumes there are.

Indeed, it may be true that the whole history of our western culture is a massive and complex version played out upon a big field of the child's game "Button, button, who's got the button?" For look at what has happened! Many hands in the history of our culture have held what they thought to be the answer to man's problems, or the way to the answer, or the kind of thoughtful labor or procedure which could bring solutions. One can quickly review in his mind some of the hands that have held the button. They constitute in their dedication and their labor our common western tradition. Think of the haunting music of Dante, in which he held all things to be completely in the hands of, and bound together by "a love that holds a sun in the heaven to all the other stars." And then the button passed on through Bruno, Nicholas of Cusa, and Galileo, to the writers of the Enlightenment who wrote discourses on the human understanding. Bacon said, "let us put aside the puerile speculations of the philosophers and let us live steadily among things." Some centuries of living fairly steadily among things does not support quite the same exuberance that Bacon could bring to that prospect. Then came the great nineteenth-century passage of the button to the historian, who envisioned the possibility of so systematic an understanding of historical process that men should be supplied with a guide to life.

It really hasn't worked out. The present custodians of the button, to be sure, are making their considerable contributions to our life. They are also making a remarkable contribution to the problematic. I quote only one, Professor Bridgeman of Harvard, who says, "We now know enough to know that there is no necessary connection between the thought in our mind and the way things are." This liberation, then, is not a liberation into secured solution or the way to it, but into life-long residence among the problematic of all liberation.

And, finally, the second question: "What is the moral stance appropriate to, indeed required by, that position, if this be the way things are?" By moral stance I mean something more than merely intellectual. I mean a totality posture in the midst of a problematic of ultimate character. Mr. Robert Oppenheimer came close to what I am reaching for in his epigram, "Style is the deference that action pays to uncertainty." This is what I mean by the style of a moral stance. Whatever that style might be, let it be suggested from *this* place, which has its own tradition of life's problematic. Let it be suggested primarily from *here* and not wait for the Dean of the College to say that these days will require an order of moral courage and an order of moral sophistication that perhaps no other generation has had to bring to this task. And instead of speaking elaborately about this, I end with what I think is a beautiful illustration.

The year is 1066. The event is the Norman conquest —which is usually reported to us in the high school books in the vulgar language of a success story. But the real Norman story is otherwise. And remember that the *jongleur* who went out ahead of the battle line and sang the inspiriting song to the warriors on that day most probably had as his ballad text the greatest of all French epics "La Chanson de Roland." The text in that battle song is not a song about Roland, the conqueror; it is rather about a man of courage who was *not* a conqueror but remained a man of courage in the midst of the unconquered. There is a modern version of that text done by Mr. Scott Moncrieff, and the introduction to it was written by Mr. Gilbert Chesterton. I want to read you a paragraph taken from the introduction in which he summarizes for us what he thinks to be the moral point of the poem.

> *That high note of a forlorn hope of a host at bay and a battle against odds without end is the note upon which the great French epic ends. I know nothing more moving in poetry than that strange and unexpected ending, that strangely inconclusive conclusion.*

Charlemagne has established his empire in quiet, he has done justice, and he sleeps upon his throne with a peace almost like that of Paradise. Just then appears to him the Angel of God crying aloud that his arms are needed in a new and distant land, that he must take up again the endless march of his days. And the great king tears his long white beard and cries out against his restless life. And thus the poem ends with a vision of war against the barbarians, and that vision is true. For that war is never ended which defends the sanity of the world against all the stark anarchies and the rending negations which rage against it forever and the grass is yet green on the graves of our friends who fell in it.

Courage, then, in the unsolved that may be insoluble, steadfastness in a life whose problematic character is a pattern and not just a phase—that is the kind of courage in which is fused both the vision of faith and the right function of a university. And that you may see the situation, know that you are not alone in it, find it possible to gain courage—this is your university's tough and affectionate wish to you upon the first Sunday of the term.

Why Do I Have To Be *Me?*

By Theodore O. Wedel
Honorary Canon, National Cathedral

I am choosing as a text this morning one of the familiar phrases in one of our Morning Prayer canticles, the one known as the Jubilate—"O be joyful in the Lord, all ye lands: serve the Lord with gladness and come before his presence with a song. Know ye that the Lord he is God: it is He that hath made us and not we ourselves."

I call your particular attention to the second verse, "Know ye that the Lord he is God: it is He that hath made us and not we ourselves."

Observers of child life can tell us that one of the earliest philosophical or religious questions asked by the growing boy or girl is "Who am I?" It is a question which may remain unanswered throughout life. A centenarian can still ask it. Indeed, this question leads to a question on an even deeper level of mystery. We ask not only "Who am I?" but "Why am I?" Or, to put it in climactic form and to phrase it colloquially: "Why do I have to be *me?*" "Why am I what I am?" "Why am I not someone else?"

The mystery of creation, of how the universe, including you and me, came into existence can puzzle all experts. But, however an answer is attempted—by the atheist or agnostic as he assigns the first cause to meaningless Fate of Chance, or by the man of religious faith with his belief in a Creator God—one simple fact stands clear. We did *not* create ourselves. We had no

11

choice in the creative act which brought us onto the stage of human life. Thrown, as it were, into existence and given the strange and mysterious endowment of self-consciousness by no choice of our own, we are simply *here*. In addition we know ourselves to be somehow responsible for what now we do with this "I" or "Me." Is it gift, or is it burden?

Here and there a man or woman may be found who is satisfied with what Fate or Chance or God has thus hurled into the maelstrom of ongoing history. But such satisfaction is surely rare. If it were a universal experience, envy and jealousy would be banished from our common life, and we should see a return of the Garden of Eden. Alas, we do envy our neighbors. We do ask, "Why do I have to be me?" "Why was I born in a humble village of the windswept plains of Kansas, a portion of the globe barren of historical significance, instead of in a famous country estate in Virginia?" "Why was I given an ugly nose instead of the features of the campus Apollo or Hollywood hero?" "Why, supposing that I am known as a handsome cavalier, did whoever hurled me into the world not give me brains as well? Or, conversely, supposing that I do have a scholar's gifted mind, why am I awkward at a dance and a Sad Sack at a party?"

This questioning of the created order and our place in it once received classic expression in one of the sonnets of Shakespeare. He is describing a mood and situation when things have gone wrong with circumstance and fate—a mood which comes upon all of us, sooner or later.

> When in disgrace with fortune and men's eyes,
>   I all alone beweep my outcast state,
> And trouble deaf heaven with my bootless cries,
>   And look upon myself and curse my fate,
> Wishing me like to one more rich in hope,
>   Featur'd like him, like him with friends possess'd,
> Desiring this man's art, and that man's scope,
>   With what I most enjoy contented least. . . .

But whenever the question "Why do I have to be me?" arises in heart of mind, do we realize what we are really saying? We are expressing, though we may not be aware of the awesome fact, hatred of the power that created us. We are rebelling against God. "It is he that hath made us and not we ourselves," and we do not like his handiwork. He is to blame, and we refuse to forgive him for what he has done to us.

This hatred of the power that hath made us as we are concerns, first of all, the circumstances that surround us—place of birth, economic condition of family or group, our biological inheritance. I can hurl maledictions on my Creator on these scores. When there is added the result of my own decisions in the form of a burden of guilt, this hatred can include myself as creator also. Man can hate both God and himself.

This rebellion can assume many forms. I venture to describe briefly three such ways of rebellion.

The first is the most familiar. It is the attempt to lose this "me" which I do not like in the life of the senses. I may try, for example, to drown it in alcohol. I can forget myself, for a little while at least, in a world of dreams. I shall not be here very long anyway. Why should I take this vanishing "I" or "me" very seriously? Let us eat, let us drink, for tomorrow we die. The results of this way of rebellion will receive no full analysis here. Skid Row or the boredom of the luxury hotel—there is not much to choose. We have a whole book in our Bible which sings the doom of this way of escape. "Vanity of vanities, all is vanity, says the Preacher."

The second way of rebellion against the Creator is the equally ancient way of the Stoic. I did not create myself, it is true. Blind Fate has me in its iron grip. This Power, however, will be fooled. I possess a citadel in my will which neither god nor devil can conquer. I am, in final trial, captain of my fate. I am master of my soul. I can be my own god, the creator of my own destiny. I can defy the power of the very stars. I can even, by way of climactic defiance, commit suicide. I did not time my beginning, but I can time my end. It is, indeed, a fact of history that suicide has been a kind of last sacrament of the Stoic from the days of the Roman emperors to our own.

Stoicism, we can readily confess, has its moral heros. There is quite possibly no rival to Christianity more appealing. It is again today a fashionable creed under the name of atheist existentialism. To defy the universe, to defy Fate—be this under the rule of God or only a blind chance, rebellion, and self-deification can go no farther.

But the Stoic faith, like all idolatry, finds a broken idol at the end of the road. No human being is great enough to play god for very long. Even the suicide cannot escape the fear that the Power which had creation under control may refuse to hand over control of the end of existence also. The Bible might still speak truth: "Know ye that the Lord he is God."

A third form of rebellion against the Creator can be tried. "Why do I have to be me?" Perhaps, after all, I don't. I can turn myself into another "I" or "me." I can pretend. I can wear a mask. I can try the art of imitation. I can obey the siren voices of the advertiser on my TV set and transform myself into a glamour girl or man of distinction by buying the right cosmetics or the right clothes or by drinking the right whiskey. Erich Fromm, one of our leading psychological specialists, has coined a striking phrase to describe this escape from reality and this rebellion against our created self. The phrase is "the commercial self." Thousands of men and women are selling their birthright as persons in their own created dignity so as to become sham merchandise on the market.

Do I need to describe the revenge which life provides for this rebellion against Him "who made us and not we ourselves"? To play a bit with the analogy of the mask—to wear a disguise at a ball may be innocent fun, but to compel the self to wear it in broad daylight and even in sleep so as not to give the secret away can turn into intolerable slavery. The real Creator God has been replaced by an idol. And idol worship, as the histories of religion can illustrate freely, demands victims—human sacrifice, no less. Dante, in describing the hypocrites in his *Inferno*, pictures them as staggering in utter weariness under a covering of lead. "O weary mantle for eternity," he cries, in pity over such a fate.

Only three attempts of rebellion against man's Creator have here received brief description. There are others, but these may suffice. They may serve as backdrop for the Gospel, for the way of life of the Christian.

"Why do I have to be me?" "Can I not be somebody else?" One answer found in Christianity may seem at first a very harsh one. No, you cannot be someone else. You cannot even, says Jesus, by being anxious add one cubit to your stature. You cannot be your own god. "Know ye that the Lord he is God: it is He that hath made us and not we ourselves." You can, to be sure, turn to idols and woo them to offer escape from your created "I." But they will let you down. You are an actor on a stage and in an action whose direction is in another's hands. You may rebel against your role. You may try to write a plot of your own invention, but the play will have a short run.

But there is one way out. It looks impossible or foolish or even cowardly at first. It is the way of submission and surrender. It is the miracle that happens when an actor, in place of rebelling against his role, accepts it as a gift. He is free at last from the burden of escape from self. He can take off his mask and the weary mantle of pretense. He can accept himself. The Christian Gospel will even tell him that he can forgive himself and shed the further burden of guilt for which man as creator of his own destiny has become responsible and which results in hatred of self as well as of God.

Such surrender is never easy. The Bible uses bold language to describe it. It is learning to pray to the Creator God, "Thy will be done, not ours." The New Testament will call this a dying—a dying even realistically symbolized in the sacramental action called Baptism—a dying which, however, has the promise of a rising again. Christians cherish a saying of the Christ: He who loseth his life shall find it. To enter the Christian life involves, so it seems, a kind of suicide. Stoic hero and Christian convert share this sacrament of surrender. The Christian's dying, however, is joyous suicide, different in kind from the bitter hate-filled defiance of the Stoic rebel against God.

Indeed the answer of NO to the question "Why do I have to be me?" or "Can I not be somebody else?" was only half-true. Christianity can also reply: Yes, you can receive a new self. In the Bible we meet again mysterious words. It speaks of being born again. It speaks of becoming a new creature in Christ Jesus. Christianity's demand for the surrender of the self to its Creator is, however, not surrender to a tyrant deity. It is surrender to a Father, or, as it can be even more boldly phrased, surrender to a Lover. The story of Revelation of the Bible is precisely a love story—the Creator wooing his rebellious children to love Him in return. It is the breathtaking epic of God Himself visiting man and breaking his proud self-will by dying for him on a cross.

Nor does the wooing end with the story of the Christ during his earthly life. As a legacy of that life there exists in the world a society called the Church, a society of the surrendered and reborn. To cite once more the strange yet wonderful language of Christian faith, those who have entered the new relationship with the Creator God through Christ speak of themselves as having died with him and then risen with him.

And in this fellowship of the newborn the question with which this sermon began is answered. "Why do I have to be me?" "Why should I accept myself as I am?" Because otherwise you will miss the wonder and glory of being loved for what you are and as you are. Here, in the company of the repentant and the forgiven, you do not have to fear rejection of yourself as you are. You can take off your mask. Even if what is revealed behind the mask is ugly—so ugly that you cannot bear the sight and cry out in shame for a hiding place and search madly for the discarded mask, there is One who can endure the sight. It is the very God who has made you. Indeed, there is a fellowship which can endure the sight. All were once in rebellion but suffered broken pride under the wooing of Christ in a manger and on a cross, entered into the joy of surrender, and are now a fellowship of prodigal sons returned to a Father's home, rejoicing in a banquet together. Here is a fellowship which, in the face of tragedy and fate, of suffering and death, can sing the *Jubilate*:

> O be joyful in the Lord all ye lands: serve the Lord with gladness, and come before his presence with a song.

> Be ye sure that the Lord he is God: it is he that hath made us, and not we ourselves; we are his people, and the sheep of his pasture.

> O go your way into his gates with thanksgiving, and into his courts with praise; be thankful unto him, and speak good of his Name.

It may seem strange to end a Christian sermon with a quotation from the Mohammedan Koran. But that classic of the religion of Islam contains more than one insight inspired by prophetic wrestling with eternal truth. The quotation reads as follows: "From God there is no flight, but unto Him." A modern poet has taken this jewel phrase and has added two further lines. The resulting triplet reads like a summary of the parable of Prodigal Son, greatest of parables in our New Testament:

> From God there is no flight, but only unto
>   Him.
> Against a father's sternness no revolt avails,
> A child's sole refuge is within his arms.

On Doing Justice and Seeking Truth

By E. Spencer Parsons
The University of Chicago

On the state capitol of California in Sacramento are inscribed these words, "God give us men to match these mountains." During the closing years of the seventh century B.C. a young prophet in Jerusalem by the name of Jeremiah was also looking for a particular kind of man. He had been commended to find a man who "does justice and seeks truth." Such men were rare during that period of Judah's history.

While we must acknowledge that history shapes men, we also know that there are men who by their singular stature bend the course of history. In the desperate days of 1940, when it looked as though nothing could stop the onrush of Hitler's troops and the relentless power of his air force, Winston Churchill raised his voice in eloquent defiance against the enemy. His words gave hope though he could promise only "blood, tears, toil and sweat." The course of the war, however, was radically altered because of the courage and fortitude of this one man.

What was Jeremiah's problem? His voice was likewise eloquent, but his message was consistently rejected. As Stanley Hopper of Drew University has said of him, "He was hurled into the time of Judah's last catastrophe." A man of valiant courage, he identified Judah's enemies and her peril without equivocation. Against the pro-Egyptian factions in the government and all who vacillated in their allegiance to Babylon, he appeared as a prophet of doom and defeatism. Because he criticized openly the foreign policies of Josiah and Jehoiakim, and because he dared to see a connection between the immorality and injustice within Judah's national life and her foreign intrigues, he was charged with treason, imprisoned, and finally carried off against his will to Egypt after the fall of Jerusalem in 586 B.C. It was no more popular to be critical of the foreign policy or the military entanglements of one's government then than in 1965!

Jeremiah saw the fall of the Assyrian empire and the rise of a neo-Babylonian empire under a Chaldean dynasty, the intrigue of Egypt's Pharoah, Neco, and the idolatry and injustices within the gates of Jerusalem as of one piece. Jeremiah saw the religious reforms of Josiah, which were based upon a new sense of obedience to the requirements of the Deuteronomic law, become superficial and shallow. To his sorrow he saw nothing substantial happen to alter the basic apostasy and self-centeredness of the people. Religious revivals apparently find it easier to settle for outward changes than to suffer through to the agonizing reorientation of one's personal and social existence. Liturgical reform always runs the risk of being an exercise in calisthenics and rhetoric at the expense of what Jeremiah and Jesus would have regarded as the weightier matters of the law.

These were the words which came to Jeremiah, "Run to and fro through the streets of Jerusalem, look and take note! Search her squares to see if you can find a man, one who does justice and seeks truth." Jeremiah did as he was commanded, and when he could not find such a man in the streets, he attributed it to the fact that the disinherited of the streets could not be expected to know the "law of their God." He then said, "I will go to the great and will speak to them; for they know the way of the Lord, the law of their God." But, he discovered, they too had broken the yoke, "they had burst the bonds."

For those of us living in this era of turbulence, Jeremiah's experience is a solemn warning. The modern American university stands in the midst of both a social and an intellectual revolution, and the word of the Lord comes to us, even as it did to Jeremiah: search the streets, the midways, the plazas, the business establishments and the churches, the halls of learning and civic centers for men who do justice and seek truth. These two stipulations are as indispensable to our survival in this century as they were to the security of Jerusalem in the seventh century B.C. Finding men to match the requirements of this day is not easy.

Universities have seldom been known for their sensitivity or courage in matters of social justice. The silence of the German universities and the churches during the rise of Nazism remains as one of the enigmas of contemporary history. In recent days some students and faculty members have dared to protest the course of events in Viet-Nam. During the past few years students, teachers, and clergyman have given leadership to the civil-rights movement. Impatient with an education which seems to focus on academic concerns too far removed from the struggle for social justice, many have marched in courageous defiance against the Bull Connors of our time. They have been arrested when asking for a cup of coffee and have been handed stones for bread. For most professors, however, the paths between their homes and their studies are well trodden, but the challenges of the social revolution of our time are met with such comments as, "I really haven't had time to follow the developments, you know!" Their response reminds me of a missionary in Africa a few years ago who was asked what the feelings of the people of his province were to the rising tide of nationalism in Africa. He replied, "I've been so busy I haven't had time to talk to the natives"! Let it be understood that the man of learning who fails to do justice in a revolutionary age is a useless fossil on the landscape of civilization.

One of the reasons why there is a growing restlessness among the students of this generation in contrast to their more docile predecessors of the fifties is that their four years of study seem disconnected from the significant issues of our common life. The academic underground—that group of "sometime" students which has become disengaged from the mainstream of academic life—will not be easily dealt with until the educational process bears a more dynamic relationship to the issues of social justice.

This, however, is only one half of the problem. Jeremiah reminds every one of us that the man who does justice must be the man who seeks truth. Truth is an evasive word, and yet, I believe, we do not have to become as cynical as Pilate. The word still points to experience in the life of man which has meaning.

Truth encompasses the search for an explanation of the compli-
cated processes of the physical world. It includes the disciplined
exploration of the tangled patterns of human behavior, and it
includes an examination and systematic delineation of the "great
ideas" which have shaped our civilization.

We know, however, that Jeremiah would not have
been satisfied simply with a descriptive, objective analysis of
problems and processes. For him and the biblical tradition generally, truth was more than propositional, more than accurate
description, more than the precise balancing of an equation in
logic or in the laboratory. It included a wisdom about existence
which was incarnate within the phenomenon of the human
person. Both the Old and the New Testaments are far more
existential in their approach to life than the idealists and moral-
ists of our Western world have been willing to admit.

Jesus was hailed as "the way, the truth and the life"
not because he measured up to the expected standards of personal achievement or because he represented in his manner and
person those public virtues of propriety and respectability which
were so hallowed by public opinion in that ancient world. Jesus
became the Christ of human experience because there were no
categories which could adequately account for him. In him, truth
became vividly and powerfully personal and not propositional.
In him, life was reshaped into a "new being." The substantial
reality of his life turned upside down the popular image of the
meaning of human life. Jeremiah was not asked to find a man
whose mind was a warehouse of facts and information, but rather
one who viscerally embodied the pilgrimage into living truth.
Any truth which does not qualify man's understanding of his
existence or have the possibility of altering the conditions of his
life is meaningless.

Our problem is not that we do not know enough; we
already know far more than is necessary for responsible living.
Our problem is a failure of commitment. Jeremiah would have
said it was fundamentally a problem of obedience. We are unwilling to risk the best that we know in the crucible of history's
conflicts. We know that economic destitution and all of its at-
tending evils cannot be helped by military power, but we still find
it easier to send military units into South Viet-Nam than risk

other avenues for the solution of problems indigenous to the area. It is easier to do nothing about slum housing and substandard education than to vote for bond issues, to fight the blight that infects our cities. It is easier to do things for other people than to help them do it themselves.

As members of this academic community we are called upon to "do justice and to seek truth." Neither one apart from the other is adequate to save our time from disaster. To be quite specific: the burden of life in Woodlawn is the burden of those who enjoy the privileges of Hyde Park and Kenwood. We are not the residents of an island but fellow citizens with others in an area of metropolitan Chicago which suffers from deep and serious wounds. Provincialism in the midst of an urban culture is a bankrupt way of approaching our common life in the decades ahead. There are some of us who believe that the decisions which are made in the next weeks with respect to the future of secondary education in Hyde Park, Kenwood, Woodlawn, and South Shore will largely determine the future health and welfare of Chicago's South Side.

The resources of the city, of the federal government, and of this university must be coordinated in such a way as to bring life and health to our neighbors to the immediate north and south of us. Not only must students continue to express their concern through SWAP and STEP; not only must the university's Department of Education move ahead with its proposed experimental school in Woodlawn, but other members of the faculty and administration must be willing to give more than lip service to the vision of a city without walls in which our diversities are accepted and respected and in which peace and justice are the guardians of our common welfare. The achievement of the good society demands that we be persons committed not only to the idea of justice, but that we be persons who do justice. Painfully this means at times that we must contribute what wisdom and resources we may have to the solution of the great human problems at our doorstep rather than always volunteering or investing our energies in projects of national and international prestige. If the churches have been guilty of a foreign mission complex to the exclusion of their responsibilities to their neighbors next door, how much more are we guilty of over-looking the cry of the neglected child and the sigh of the unemployed father who live only blocks from our comfortable homes and dormitories.

One final word about Jeremiah's requirement that the man who does justice be the man who seeks truth. One of the temptations of our technological culture is to assume that the truth about life can only be grasped rationally by the objective observer. Certainly some valuable understandings can be achieved by such methods, but other truths will be discovered and indeed created only by risking commitment. Love and concern and forgiveness are realities which give life its most profound meaning. To serve another's deepest need, to stand in faithfulness to another's humanness, to forgive another's injury mean more to the dignity and health of human personality than all the technical accomplishments of which our society can boast.

Jesus said in the gospel of John, "If you continue in my word, you are truly my disciples, and you will know the truth, and the truth will make you free." This passage never assumed that the accumulation of facts and figures, of propositions, or of effective techniques for controlling the universe would make us free. What the members of the early Church discovered through their own experience was that when life was viewed in the light of what Jesus said and did and what he was in the power of his self-hood, then they became men and women who were free to love and serve and suffer and rejoice and die, when before they had been anxious and hesitant and timid in their self-centeredness.

The new creation which John visualized in the Book of Revelation pointed to a time when the thirsty would be given "water without price from the fountain of life." Such a vision depends upon our developing a new style of life which bears a more consistent relationship to the vision of the prophets and the image of the Christ in the New Testament. This final assurance comes to us from the last book of the Bible—"He who conquers shall have this heritage, and I will be his God and he shall be my son." This is the biblical promise, and its confidence is not unrelated to our deepest needs.

A Public Example

By Gibson Winter
The University of Chicago

> *He disarmed the principalities and powers and made*
> *a public example of them, triumphing over them in*
> him.
>
> —Colossians 2:15

The paradox of our religious situation is the momentous character of the public responsibilities that press upon us and the increasingly private scope of our religious concerns. Indeed, this paradox is manifest through the whole range of American culture, for withdrawal from public responsibility into autonomous enclaves has characterized our national life since World War II.

To this extent, the private character of our religious understanding—the pietistic focus upon personal salvation, personal faith, inner emotional stability, personal *integrity,* and a host of other private aspects of life—only reflects a retreat from the public sphere and, to this extent, from the Gospel.

Retreat to privacy is, of course, a familiar phenomenon in the face of crisis. Many survivors of the German purge of the Jewish people have recounted how their families gathered for music recitals in the parlor while their synagogues were being burned by gangs in the neighboring blocks. Similarly, many Jewish families found it impossible to assess the full seriousness of the impending destruction; they simply could not face such a future realistically. Thus, retreat to privacy is an understandable reaction to a threatening future, but it radically impairs one's capacity to cope realistically with the present.

To be sure, stress on the private character of religion has a long tradition in the United States; in fact, most Americans read the Scriptures as though they were written to endorse American individualism with the assurance of individual salvation. Consequently, our widespread anxiety about the future, our retreat to privacy, is simply reinforcing this private interpretation of Christianity.

Our text from Colossians, and innumerable other texts which might be cited, contrasts radically with this private interpretation of the work of Jesus as the Christ. The event of the Crucifixion-Resurrection—and this is the event which we mean by Gospel—is the decisive struggle between the sovereign Lord and the demonic powers which have enslaved the world. This is a cosmic event; its significance is universal. To be sure, these demonic powers impinge upon the inward life of the person, and the public triumph over them will have significant effects on personal integrity, but neither the context of the event nor the scope of its effects can be properly understood in terms of an individual search for fulfilment or integrity.

The future has become problematic for the people of the United States. We have moved beyond the childish confidence of former periods of our history. We have moved into the maturity which reckons with the future as limit and possibility. We have entered history as people who know themselves to be responsible within history.

When the future becomes problematic, a mature Gospel can be proclaimed; moreover, the metaphor of history, with its categories of past, present, and future, proves a creative vehicle for appropriating this Gospel. The historical maturity of man opens depth dimensions for authentic religious encounter, even as this maturity of modern man transforms the terms in which the Gospel can be grasped. We can think today in terms of a Gospel about public events and meanings. We can consider our victory over the principalities which enslave us. We can envision the cosmic work of Christ.

The nature of the principalities is revealed, to some extent, in the struggle between the university and The Woodlawn Organization during the past few years. When the New Testament speaks of principalities, it means demonic powers which come into play as men wrestle with their future. Both the University of Chicago and the Woodlawn area are struggling desperately with the question as to whether they have any future. This struggle has broad significance, for it mirrors in one locale a struggle which is going on in every metropolitan area of the United States. It is, indeed, the life-or-death struggle of the emerging metropolis. We can phrase the issue in these words: Can our cities become a human environment for personal growth and cultural development? Does a university with the great tradition for learning of the University of Chicago have any future in Chicago or in any other American city? Do the people of the Woodlawn area have any hope for a human life in this metropolis?

When the future becomes problematic, when it is in doubt, a host of destructive forces come into play—perhaps the most prominent being the attempt to control the future by sheer power. Of course, power and particular interests come into play wherever there is human action, but reliance upon sheer financial or mass power—exclusive concentration upon the achievement of one's own interests—is the attempt to make the future dependent upon one's present power and needs. This belief in power, this credo of self-interest, taken by itself, provokes a chain of conflicting interests and powers, ultimately reducing a neighborhood or international situation to sheer anarchy. This was precisely Hitler's effect upon the world—naked power provokes power. We are on the verge of anarchy in this situation, although there are signs that the university has awakened to a much more realistic sense of its *common* future with Woodlawn—to the knowledge that no amount of sheer power can give us a future.

Whatever the faults and guilt in the past relationship between these two structures, and the university certainly helped to provoke The Woodlawn Organization, these powers only have a future *together* and that means a future in the context of the interests and possibilities of the whole metropolis of Chicago.

The future can never be built simply upon particular power and domination, for there are ever new forms of power provoked by such an attempt to possess the future on one's own terms. Innumerable groups have arisen in recent years in an attempt to control the future by defining it in terms of their own interests and by dominating all groups who threaten those interests. Some of these groups have been polite and have employed the velvety techniques of the middle class. Others have been violent and ugly. There is some justification for the interests of most of these groups. Usually they are rightly fearful over what the future holds. There is no future for them, however, when this future is defined by their own domination. Chicago will be uninhabitable if organizations like The Woodlawn Organization or the Southeast Chicago Commission simply dominate the situation by realizing their own power and by responding with hostility to every threat. Each of these groups may and should legitimately represent its particular interests in the public forum, but only as these interests are defined in terms of our common future as a community—living together in mutual concern for the human environment of the whole metropolis; only in this context of a future over which neither group has control will there be a future for either group. This is a lesson Germany had to learn in recent years. It is the lesson that the white citizens councils have yet to learn. The fear of the future which manifests itself as power and hatred is the principality which enslaves and destroys —closing off any *real* future and substituting an illusory future built upon exploitation.

The Woodlawn Organization, with all its demonic potentialities and its fundamental misconception of the nature of human community and history, has invoked, nevertheless, a decisive truth of the Gospel which the churches had forgotten, that is, that the sphere of the Gospel is the public sphere of human struggle for a future. The churches of Woodlawn have brought this reality of the Gospel home to all the churches—pastorate is pastorate to a whole community, not to an enclave. These same churches will have to transmute the power structures of The Woodlawn Organization into a suitable instrument for shaping a human future in the metropolis for all people, Negro and white, Latin American and North American. The struggle with the principalities is not a dirty business to be carried on by others, something for the politicians. It is precisely the work of the churches, but the churches are not to identify themselves with these principalities and their hatreds, for then men are surely damned and left without a future. We need not fear the principalities! We need not justify them!

Cynical voices on both sides of the Woodlawn-university struggle repeatedly define the situation simply in terms of interests and power. These are the voices which are enslaved to the principalities, feeding upon them like parasites, evoking fear and hatred where possible, and rejoicing in evil and destruction. We can sympathize with these poor creatures because there is an illusory sense of being alive, even though they are dead—that is, have no future—they play upon people's fear of the future and grasp for the future, foment crises, and rush from here to there in a mad desire to prove that they are really significant. But the principalities are not overcome in this way; one does not triumph over them in serving them, for they constrain us to ever-increasing submission. One has no future in bondage to these powers, for these powers arise from fear of the future and man's attempt to control the future on his own terms.

Triumph over the principalities—leading them captive, making them a public example—can never be done by serving one's own interests. Domination over others does not conquer these powers, for they lure men with the promise of domination. The future is the community of man in which we belong together, what the Gospel calls the Kingdom, and only those who belong to this future overcome the destructive forces of these principalities in the present.

Incidents in Atlanta, Georgia, this past year give ample testimony to the power of the future which the Gospel calls the Kingdom and give witness to the triumph of this future over the principalities. Students from Morehouse College and young men and women from the adjoining colleges started a sit-in last year in order to open the lunch counters in the department stores. A good many of them were arrested and stayed in jail while the Negro community boycotted all the goods stores.

After some months, the mothers became fearful that the students would miss out on a year's education and sent a delegation urging them to come out on bail. The spokesman for the students said that they could not come out, knowing that their own children would have to be in that jail some day because they could not stick it. The students knew that the boycott would collapse the moment they came out of jail, for the boycott was in good part a protest against the jailing of the young men and women, not to mention the beatings to which many of them were subjected in the course of the strikes.

These young people had a grasp on the future which made it possible for them to shape the present creatively. They could use the forces of fear which had jailed them as a public means to overcome the discrimination and segregation this fear had created, for they used their captivity to overcome the segregation of the lunch counters. They used the principalities and powers as a means to their common future in equality with the white community. This is not to say that there is never a time to fight, but only that, even when it comes to fighting, the future must be seen as a common future or it is no future, for the Kingdom is our common humanity under God.

When one compares the forces of fear and hatred in the southern white community with the courage and patience of the Negro community, it is obvious who has a future. The white community is largely captive to its own fear, dealing out death and destruction, attempting to foreclose the future of the Negro community. It is perfectly clear who has a future, for the Negro community belongs so utterly to this future that they have the most realistic kind of present—they can deal wisely with the whites. The department store owners, on the other hand, showed how unrealistic one's dealing with the present becomes when one fears the future. In fear, we fall back upon formulas from the past which are irrelevant. The department store owners called in some of the mothers and treated them rather politely, showing them some completely remodeled rest rooms that would now be available to the Negro women. When it was pointed out to the owners that the little sign above the rest room saying "Colored Only" would have to be removed, the owners were very hurt and felt that the Negro women were being ungrateful. Fear of the future, like the attempt to control the future, destroys the present, so that we deal with an illusory present on the basis of past, lifeless formulas. It is in this sense that the law becomes destructive of the present. The law becomes a defense against the unpredictable future—and the law is unto death.

There is a world of difference between the perspective of the students in Atlanta and the philosophies that have guided Woodlawn and the University of Chicago, for the Atlanta students sacrifice their own claims on behalf of a common humanity. These students are not setting their own interests above the community to which they all belong. They are not simply engaging in a struggle for domination over against the white community. Whoever won such a struggle would have no future, for there is no true future outside the common humanity to which we are summoned. The students have been able to bend the powers of fear, guilt, and hatred back upon themselves, using the force exerted against them by this fear as a means to triumph over that fear. This victory in the present is not won by mass power or a struggle to maintain particular interests; these students have sacrificed their own interests for a common life which they will only glimpse from afar but never fully share. Their children may now enter into this inheritance. Striking, picketing, use of group pressure, and even the use of violence if necessary are not in themselves wrong. The decisive question is the end and consequences as well as the motivational forces which are invoked in the action. The principalities and powers exploit conflicts of interest in order to fan hatred and arouse struggle for private interests. Against these powers, only those who belong to the future, committed to a common humanity and dedicated to subordinate all means to this future, only these can make the principalities a public example, triumphing over them. The struggle with these powers is won neither by a religious life that turns to personal privacy nor by identifying with these powers as religious forces. Only the future which we cannot possess—the future coming to us as gracious gift—can free us from the guilt and fear which enslave us to these powers. There was no question in Atlanta who was afraid, who guilty, who had no future. There was no question who had a future, for it was that future impinging upon the present which transmuted the powers of fear into an instrument of reconciliation. Here we are close to the heart of the Gospel, for these students re-enacted that enpowering event which we call Gospel—the life-giving and healing sacrifice.

Even a superficial reading of the New Testament brings home the fact that Jesus' followers, friends, and family became more and more convinced that he had little future. In a paradoxical way, the principalities saw his future. It was evident to the threatened interests among the Romans, to the guilt of the Pharisees, and to the fear of the temple authorities. In a cunning way, the principalities redouble their fury before the true future which discloses them for what they are. Of all the destructive forces leveled against him, moreover, the most vicious was the guilt created by his holiness. Those who live by the law see its shabby claims to virtue turn to nothing before him. This fury to vindicate the past (and the law is the past) treated as the basis of our future enlists forces as vile as the Roman sword against this man. All of this he accepted—nailing this law to the cross with his own body—accepting the death to which his Father summoned him. And his Father, who summoned him to this death, raised him from it—triumphing over fear, guilt, and human pride—leading these principalities captive and using his death as a means to free men from the fear and guilt which close out their future. He took this man with no future and gave him to us as universal presence—as everyman's future. He led captivity captive and gave gifts to men—the One who had no future, who surrendered his future on behalf of the community to which he and his persecutors belonged, becomes for all men the future —the one who bestows a future upon man—the giver of life through death.

2

FAITH CONFRONTS
SCIENCE

The Return to Nature

By *Jaroslav Pelikan*
Yale University

> *I am sure that neither death, nor life, nor angels, nor*
> *principalities, nor things present, nor things to come,*
> *nor powers, nor height, nor depth, nor anything else*
> *in all creation, will be able to separate us from the*
> *love of God in Christ Jesus our Lord.*
> —Romans 8:38–39

Anyone who tries to regulate his life both by the calendar of the university and by the calendar of the Church must confess to considerable embarrassment. This is not only because the university marks Memorial Day as a holiday on its calendar in the memory of the heroes of the Republic, but schedules classes on Good Friday; or because the week between the Winter and the Spring Quarter almost never manages to coincide with Holy Week, but also because somehow the feasts of the Church are always out of step with the rhythm of the academic year. One of the first times I preached in this chapel it was Mother's Day, which is surely no feast of the Church but seems to have been observed by the university, presumably because she is our alma mater; so I preached on the Church as our mother. A few years ago the first Sunday in the Winter Quarter also happened to be the Epiphany of our Lord, but the Wise Men from the East (and from the Middle West) do not come any more. Today is the first regular Sunday of this school year, and it comes

right after, of all things, the Christian feast day of St. Michael
and All Angels; and after Succoth, the Jewish Feast of Tabernacles.

Here is the epitome of our embarrassment: St.
Michael and All Angels day on the campus of the University of
Chicago! Seven hundred years ago that was perfectly in order;
indeed, it is almost exactly seven hundred years since St. Thomas
Aquinas, who would surely be a distinguished service professor in
any university, began to compose the *Summa* in 1265. This book,
you will remember, has much information about the habits and
the habitats of the angels, even though neither St. Thomas nor
any other medieval doctor I know anything about ever said anything about their dancing on the head of a pin. But what in the
world can we do with St. Michael and All Angels at a university
now? I would suggest that a careful study of how the early
Church treated the idea of angels gives us some leads not only to
the meaning of this question, but also to the fuller meaning of
the Gospel itself. For the ultimate meaning of the Gospel is
deliverance from the supernatural and a return to nature. It is of
this that I want to speak this morning: deliverance from the
supernatural and a return to nature. The text from the epistle
to the Romans carries us through three possible confessions
about nature and the all: (1) the all is God; (2) God is Lord
over the all; (3) the all is in God.

"The all is God." This confession of the noblest
minds of paganism summarizes the glory and the despair of the
religion of nature, past and present. Once it had become obvious
that the Divine could not be identified with the cavorting deities
on Mount Olympus, who were superior to men not in virtue but
only in endurance, men had to look for the ultimate elsewhere.
They found it in a deified nature: "the all is God." In the text
the Apostle Paul gives us a catalog of some of the principal
manifestations of this deified nature: death, life, angels, principalities, things present, things to come, powers, height, depth.
Thus men looked for the disclosure of the divine in the mysterious ebb and flow of human existence (life, death), in the succes-
sion of the time process (things present, things to come), in the

patterns of the heavenly bodies (height, depth, which were the technical terms in astrology for the celestial spaces above and below the horizon through which the stars passed), and in the teeming multitude of supernatural beings (angels, principalities, powers). Worship was a means of getting on the right side of these mysterious powers, magic a way of discerning (and perhaps of influencing) their awesome hold over human life.

The domain of the angels, then, was the realm of the supernatural. Yes, they touched the natural world now and again as they swooped by in their celestial orbits, but the line was drawn between nature and supernature, and the angels belonged to supernature. When nature is deified, the terrors and the hopes in which men live attach themselves to the natural yet supernatural beings who people the atmosphere. Therefore, the text speaks of death and life, height and depth, for it is both terror and hope that the religion of nature tries to explain. It can seek the explanation in the changing of the seasons, as it did in the nature festivals, of which the Canaanite original of the Jewish Feast of Tabernacles is a prime example. It can try to find the answer in the hidden fires of sex, worshiping the natural vitalities as something supernatural; this we can see in Baal and Ashteroth, in Venus and Priapus. It can look for ultimate meaning in human death, reabsorption into the abyss of the all, and the soothing coolness of the starry night. And the little gods of the little people proved to be as accommodating as little gods always are, taking upon themselves the various features and functions of all these myths and rituals. The world into which Christianity came was a world enthralled by the supernatural, tyrannized by religion, bullied by the angels. The confession "The all is God" handed man over to a religion of nature that sought the supernatural in the unnatural and thus stood in danger of losing both the natural and the supernatural. The atheists and the skeptics were right: man had to be delivered from the supernatural; the angels had to be cut down to size.

To the confession "The all is God," Christianity opposes the confession "God is Lord over the all." That is the confession of the text. "Neither death, nor life, nor angels, nor principalities, nor things present, nor things to come, nor powers, nor height, nor depth, nor anything else in all creation, will be able to separate us from the love of God in Christ Jesus our Lord." To find what "the all" means and to know how "the all" stands in relation to the divine, we are to look, not at "the all," but at "the love of God in Christ Jesus our Lord." What happened to Christ Jesus, in his history, is the key to understanding angels, principalities, powers, height, depth, yes, even life and death. To give substance to this confession, the Christian community proclaimed the sovereignty of the Father of our Lord Jesus Christ over "the all." The world peered at the stars to trace the orbits of the gods in the sky; the Church subordinated the star to God and made it lead the Magi "till it came to rest over the place where the Child was." Some men thought that the mysteries of growth in the world of nature disclosed the meaning of life. The Church, even as it remembered the lilies of the field and the birds of the air, described the children tearing down the branches of the palms to greet Jerusalem's unknown king and described the King himself enthroned upon the tree of the cross. Supernaturalism pondered the being of the angels as a clue to the being of the universe; in the Christian faith both angels and demons took the role of the Greek chorus, commenting upon the chief events of the drama of redemption—not granting the victory of life over death, but asking the Easter mourners in God's name: "Why do you seek the living among the dead?"

The message of the Gospel, then, directs our gaze away from the supernatural and to the historical. The angels are signposts pointing to him who is the way, heralds announcing him who is the truth, fellow creatures with us celebrating him who is the life. So it was that Israel took the Canaanite festivals of nature and made them festivals of the historical convenant. The Feast of Tabernacles or Booths becomes a way of remembering, says the Torah of Moses, "that I made the people of Israel dwell in booths when I brought them out of the land of Egypt: I am the Lord your God" (Leviticus 23:43). And the Feast of Succoth closes with Sincath Torah, "rejoicing at the Law." The covenant of mercy given in the Exodus, the love of God in Christ Jesus our Lord—here the eyes of faith are summoned to see, and to obey, the word and will of God. The ancient world had ritual ablutions aplenty, though none of the soap was 99.44 per cent pure, but Christianity offered baptism into Christ, into union with his death and with his resurrection. The nations know that bread contains the life of the divine and that wine unites us with the very power of being, but Christianity remembered that our Lord took the bread and the wine in the night in which he was betrayed and made them bearers of that body and blood through which hope and salvation had come. The cross is thus the disenchantment of the world of nature, or, as the fathers of the Church said, the sign of the cross puts the demons to flight. The Gospel came to cleanse the air of deities, to shoo away the gods, to teach the angels to know their place, and to celebrate the enthronement of God—the God of the Covenant and the Father of Jesus Christ as the Lord over the all.

But the Gospel confesses "God is Lord over the all" in order to be able to confess "The all is in God." A generation ago it was fashionable, with Frazer's *Golden Bough*, to emphasize the similarities between Christianity and the ancient religions of nature-supernature: the angels were minor deities, the Jesus was the corn god. Now it is fashionable to put "the New Testament against its environment," to set Christianity against religion, and to emphasize the novelty of the Gospel so radically that I sometimes wonder how anyone in the first century could ever have understood what the apostles were talking about. As a result of this present fad, the Christian message sometimes fails to get around to this third confession, "The all is in God." Meanwhile, a new religion of nature, with its own magic and its own superstition, has become the religion of many men. It still looks to the changing of the seasons, to sex and the natural vitalities, and to the soothing coolness of the starry night as explanations of the mystery of being. Though we do not live in the Newtonian universe of Alexander Pope, many a twentieth-century man would say of himself, as Pope did:

> *Slave to no sect, who takes no private road,*
> *But looks through Nature up to Nature's God.*

And the great betrayal of Christian faith in our time is that in response to this, Christian thought fails to look through history to nature and to nature's God.

Yet that is what is meant to pull the angels back into nature. Neither death, nor life, nor angels, *nor anything else in all creation* could pose an ultimate threat to man's life in the love of God, because the angels and all that crowd belonged to the creation. The line was drawn not between the natural and the supernatural but between the creature and the Creator, in whom the creature finds its fulfilment. The study of the angels by the medieval doctors was the study of fellow creatures, not the final chapter in the history of Christian supernaturalism, but an early chapter in the history of the Christian return to nature. Indeed, I would suggest that the textbooks are all wrong—as textbooks, of course, usually are—and that the great change in the history of man's picture of the universe comes not with the so-called destruction of the Christian world view by modern man, but with the proclamation of the living God as the Creator of "the all": angels, principalities, powers, planets, and man. The issue is not the existence of angels, but the naturalness of creation. Hence the medieval view of the angels and the modern view of the universe, diametrically opposed in their methods, assumptions, and conclusions, are nevertheless part of the same outlook on a world where the power of God has prevailed over the power of the gods, the tyranny of the supernatural has been broken, and the mind of man disenthralled.

A generation ago a man who tried to be both a man of letters and a historian—and, as one who would like to be both, I can tell you that this is no easy trick—described the zenith of the process I have been talking about:

> The flowers and stars have recovered their first inno-
> cence. Fire and water are felt to be worthy to be the
> brother and sister of a saint. The purge of paganism is
> complete at last. For water itself has been washed.
> Fire itself has been purified as by fire. Water is no
> longer that water in which slaves were flung to feed

the fishes. Fire is no longer that fire through which children were passed to Moloch. Flowers smell no more of the forgotten garlands gathered in the garden of Priapus; stars stand no more as signs of the far frigidity of gods as cold as those cold fires. They are all like things newly made and awaiting new names. . . . Neither the universe nor the earth have now any longer the old sinister significance of the world. They await a new reconciliation with man, but they are already capable of being reconciled. Man has stripped from his soul the last rag of nature-worship, and can return to nature.

—G. K. Chesterton

Christian theology and preaching face no challenge today more urgent than this return to nature. For the air, once polluted with angels and demons and then purged in the name of God the Creator by the power of the cross, is being polluted again by the work of men's hands. We loot the earth, and the bucolic artificiality of life in America separates men from the very nature in which they seek refuge. Who speaks for nature and the mute creation today? In response to the need, the preaching of so many churches drones on about "Do this" and "Don't do that," or about being like Jesus, or about the menace of philosophy, science, and socialism. As though the Sanctus had not put our worship into the setting of a heaven and earth filled with the glory of God and as though the early Church had not called the cross of Christ "the healing of creation"! From nature to history, yes, and from "nature or nature's God" to the Redeemer. But then from history back to nature, and from the Redeemer to the Creator—and to the creation! For it is the love of God, of God the Creator, that is given in Christ Jesus our Lord, in whom we are called to be born into a new creation. The world today awaits and needs the Gospel of the new creation, the bold confession that all is in God, whether stars or angels or starfish or men.

I say that we are wound
With mercy round and round
As if with air . . .
Men here may draw like breath
More Christ and baffle death;
Who, born so, comes to be
New self and nobler me
In each one and each one
More makes, when all is done,
Both God's and Mary's Son.
                —Gerard Manley Hopkins[1]

[1] Reprinted from *Poems of Gerard Manley Hopkins*, edited by W. H. Gardner, published by Oxford University Press (1948).

Science and Religion in Threshold Experience

By Harold K. Schilling
Pennsylvania State University

During this period intended for meditation let us reflect upon and give thanks for one of the characteristics of man by which he is seen to be truly and uniquely human.

There was a time when man was commonly classified as "only an animal." It seems, however, that his arrival on earth is increasingly being regarded as the appearance of a new kind of being, after a long prior evolutionary development. He is considered as one who, though originally related to the animals, is in many respects radically different from them. For he turned out to be a thinker and reasoner, an inventor and fabricator, a discerner and creator of beauty.

Among man's distinctively human characteristics there is one that is especially significant for our present subject: he is the being with "threshold experience." Philip Wheelwright in his remarkable book *The Burning Fountain* speaks of threshold existence as follows:

> *Man always lives on the verge, always on the borderland of something more. . . . The intimation of something more, beyond the horizon, belongs to the very nature of consciousness. To be conscious is not just to be; it is to mean, to intend, to point beyond oneself, to testify that some kind of beyond exists and to be ever on the verge of entering it.*

In elaborating this he speaks of the threshold of time, of the world, and of the unseen. It is on the third of these that I would like us to reflect.

Living and thinking on the threshold of the unseen is by no means unusual. Nowhere is this more in evidence than in science. While, unfortunately, science is commonly thought of as being largely an enterprise in the accumulation of so-called directly perceptible facts, actually it is primarily a looking behind or beyond such facts. Science does not even begin until one has inquired into how the raw data fit together and can be explained, or by what conceptual, theoretical structures they may be seen to make sense, or what patterns of hidden reality and relationship they reveal.

Note, for example, the typical restlessness of the scientific mind evident in this series of questions: What is this? A desk. What is it made of? Lumber, nails, and glue. What are its chemical constituents, and what, in turn, are they composed of?

Science has insisted on pushing such inquiry to ever deeper levels, until it has reached that of the so-called elementary particles. As this audience is well aware, according to this conception the desk is a swarm of myriads of particles, called electrons, protons, and neutrons, which are exceedingly small and proportionately as far apart as the planets are in the solar system. The point to be emphasized for present purposes is that these successively deeper probings that have led to this remarkable picture point to a distinctively human phenomenon, namely profound dissatisfaction with knowledge of only the apparent, coupled with a powerful urge to explore the unseen behind it.

Having said this, I must add that this picture is, in certain respects, misleading and needs qualification. For one thing, the nature of the entities called electrons, protons, and neutrons is such that the term "particle" adequately symbolizes only some of their characteristics. Others are more aptly suggested by the term "wave." Therefore, to tell the whole story we should talk in terms of both particles and waves, as well as of various fields associated with them. More than that, however, we must realize that even when we make such modifications, this kind of a picture remains basically unsatisfactory because it depicts the extremely small, the unseen, by means of the imagery or concepts of the large, the seen. We now know—and this seems to me to be one of the most remarkable contributions contemporary science has made—that the physical microworld and macroworld are so radically different that thought and communication about the one requires concepts and symbols that are in important respects very different from those that are suitable for the other. This is why in physics we need an uncertainty principle and a principle of complementarity and why we minimize the use of mechanical or pictorial models in our theorizing and prefer pictorially noncommittal, mathematical ones after the manner of quantum mechanics.

This illustrates an extremely important characteristic of threshold experience in general, namely, that crossing the threshold of the unseen always seems to require changes in our ways of thinking and to require, therefore, novel language.

Science is not, however, the only human enterprise based on the threshold experience of the unseen. Another is art. Take, for instance, poetry. Did not Robert Frost remind us repeatedly that poetry is a quest into the beyond, and that in his own poems he was always using the immediate and apparent to symbolize more ultimate, veiled, ulterior meanings? Consider also the painter. Why is it that he has so much more to say to us than the photographer? Is it not because he has penetrated the realm of esthetic reality to regions that are quite inaccessible to the camera? And the musician? Would he not say that music is much more audible sound—that it is threshold experience that reveals the inaudible beyond the audible?

It cannot be stressed too much that art, like science, is a sublime human impatience with the obvious, a living on the verge of something more and a straining, reaching out for the seemingly undiscernible. And again it is to be noted that crossing the threshold requires different ways of thinking and communicating. Certainly the language of art is not at all like that of everyday life.

A third gateway experience is represented by philosophy, the search for unseen, hidden meanings. On one side of this threshold is an accumulation of established conceptions, myths, beliefs, and mores that constitute, so to speak, the visible world of the obvious and accepted notions of mankind. Along comes Socrates, who asks uncomfortable, needling questions, disturbing the status quo, and bidding us to step over the threshold into the realm of as yet unseen ideas and ways of thinking. What, he asks, do your present ideas mean? What should they mean? Are they true, or worthy, or ludicrous? Perhaps there are better ones.

But analysis and criticism are not the only functions of philosophy. Another is to be creative. And so after Socrates came Plato and Aristotle and a host of other innovators— fashioners of powerful new intellectual tools and builders of grand structures of thought. Life has been enriched immeasurably by this distinctively human threshold enterprise called philosophy.

Next we must note that universally and perennially men have felt impelled to peer even farther into the beyond and thus have found themselves at still another threshold, at which they cry out, "But why?" And this "why" is different from that of philosophy, for it is born not of curiosity of the mind so much as of perplexity and anguish of heart. What for: matter and energy, cause and effect, natural law, beauty, and rationality? What difference do they make? Is there any purpose in it all? Or moral and eternal value? Why life and death, good and evil, love and hate? This is the gateway experience of religion.

Often we confuse philosophy and religion. Though their questions often seem identical, actually they are not. Thus to ask "What is truth in general?" is manifestly different from asking what is the truth in a particular situation calling for a fateful personal decision. To ask academically "What is the meaning of death?" is not the same as asking this in the presence of a particular death of, say, a loved one. The point is that in religion questions are asked with a sense of tremendous personal significance and urgency, with what Professor Tillich calls ultimate concern, in contrast to more preliminary concerns.

Now it is at this threshold that men have become aware of transcendent reality, reality that is also transcendent mystery. And they have discovered that here the intellectual *tour de force* is of no avail, that no push of their own can get them across the threshold. Yet, eventually, many men have found themselves drawn to the other side. In spite of the inscrutability of this beyond, there comes out of it compelling revelations of another dimension of reality that they have come to call the holy or sacred, and of ultimate meaning and purpose, of a moral order. Here they have felt demands being made upon them and transforming forces and empowering energy. Moreover, in the light of the insights that have come out of this encounter, all of nature and history, as well as of personal existence, have been illumined and are seen to have aspects of meaning not discerned at other thresholds. To the source of these experiences and insights men of many races and religions have given the name God, however they may have spelled it in their various languages.

According to Judaeo-Christian conceptions, this God is not the God of philosophic abstraction, but the experienced God of Abraham, Isaac, and Jacob. For Christians he is also the Father of Jesus Christ, and thus the God who has broken into and himself experienced human existence through his incarnation. He is the living, creating, reconciling, redeeming, loving, and judging God. Typically such assertions are not to be found in philosophical treatises on the Deity.

Parenthetically let me remark that by the terms "religious experience" and "vision" I do not here refer to what is often meant by them, namely, a private, subjective, emotional experience sometimes called "getting religion" or a trancelike experience of "having a vision." Nor do I refer especially to the so-called mystic experience that makes its appearance in all high religions—and that I do not in the least derogate or challenge. Rather I am talking about the common experience that comes to ordinary people, individually and in community, when—in moments or reflection or worship, or as the result of long-range thought and study—they become aware of the presence of God in the world and in history and more particularly in their own lives, and then yield themselves to him in holy, unselfish commitment to the cause of love and justice among men.

With the coming of this understanding, the world and human existence are seen to make sense and to have purpose and value, and many persistent perplexities are resolved.

But not all of them! While in the religious threshold experience, many men and women have been vouchsafed certainty as to the reality of the unseen beyond; such certainty does not apply to all of the concepts or theological doctrines that come out of reflection upon that experience. Far from it! One reason for this is that once again men find that the thought patterns and symbols indigenous to one side of a threshold are not in themselves adequate on the other. Just as a scientific picture of the unseen microworld is inadequate if it is sketched out exclusively in terms of the imagery of the macroworld, so any symbolism drawn from finite human existence is inadequate relative to the infinite God, as, for instance, when God is spoken of without qualification as a "person" or "persons," or, for that matter, as an "impersonal force" or "influence." While in both science and religion the use of everyday language in that manner is definitely helpful and enlightening, it is nevertheless misleading in important respects and, therefore, incapable of helping us to resolve many of our perplexities. This is one reason, I take it, why Tillich has resorted to such unconventional expressions as "God above God"—that is, God beyond all man-made conceptions or symbols of "him" or "it." New language is needed here, and perhaps we should expect that none will ever be wholly adequate.

In all threshold experience of the unseen—that of science, art, philosophy, and religion—man has found much insight that is true and meaningful, but there is much also that has eluded him and refused to be captured and encased in words. Let us be humbly grateful for this, for it means that there remains much that is open for further exploration and contemplation. According to Judaeo-Christian insights, God has not made a closed world, the content and meaning of which could conceivably be exhausted some day. Rather he is the God-Becoming as well as the God-Being who continues to create, whose world is and remains open and pregnant with unseen possibilities. This is the basic reason why this university can have—and can expect to continue to have—its great festivals of scholarship and research, such as those devoted to evolution, to nuclear science, and the present one on space science. For God himself, if I may use such frankly inadequate, yet suggestive, anthropomorphic symbolism, each day becomes a threshold experience as he looks into the as yet uncreated, unseen future. In giving us the desire and capacity for adventure and creative threshold experience, he shares with us, so to speak, one of his most divine attributes— and thus enables us to be truly human. Surely this is what the Bible means in part when it asserts that man is made in his image.

The New Age

By Huston Smith
Massachusetts Institute of Technology

Twenty years ago it happened. Here, on this spot. Mind and matter, locked in the most intense and desperate embrace ever essayed, gave birth. Stagg Field was the manger. And the child? A savior-monster the like of which man heretofore could contemplate only in story. Fire, steel, and pestilence were welded into one; Prometheus, Daedalus, and Pandora incarnated as Fermi, Compton, and Zinn. And once again myth became history.

As a result we stand as new men in the face of unknown things. Turning our gaze in the arc of peril, back across the two decades that have intervened and forward toward the road ahead, what shall we say? What is the word for that day and this, the sermon for this score of years? How shall we use these dangling hands, these words that draw us on like dreams?

First, surely, for praise. For we are still here—a fact which in itself is a near-miracle. Considering the tensions that have riven our world and the destruction they could so easily have brought down upon us, our presence is a tribute—to God or man, as you choose, probably to both. But what after praise?

The light of an exploding atomic bomb is said to appear brighter than a thousand suns. The interesting question is, Has its flash thrown any light on the *human* situation? Against the backdrop of the mushroom cloud does man stand silhouetted more distinctly?

50

I propose that we ponder this question through five thoughtful comments on our new age.

The first comes through Robert Oppenheimer. Deep within the solitary wastes of New Mexico's deserts on the morning of July 16, 1945, he stood witness to the first test bomb which he had himself so largely engineered. As he watched the tremendous light envelop the heavens, followed by the deep growling roar, two lines from the Bhagavad-Gita flashed across his mind:

> I am become death,
> The shatterer of worlds.

Or, as another translation has it:

> I am come as Time, the waster of peoples,
> Ready for that hour that ripens to their ruin.

Peril. Peril unprecedented. This was the age's first and obvious disclosure. Or rather reminder, for early man had known life's precariousness. Crouched at his campfire, circled by beasts of prey, early man knew well what it was to live facing the yawning jaws of destruction. But we had forgotten. The insulations of science—against cold through central heating, against famine through granaries, against disease through medicines— had bred illusions of security in us. Suddenly the props were removed, and again we saw ourselves where, in fact, man's life has always been—suspended by a thread over 70,000 fathoms.

There is a wisdom which says that to be aware of life's precariousness is a gain. It is the wisdom which asks us to think how we would live the remaining hours of any day if we knew that they were to be our last. The wisdom that understands how confrontation with death can dissolve the pettiness, pretense, selfishness, and superficiality which characterize so much of our normal unthinking years. "So teach us to number our days that we may apply our hearts unto wisdom." Teach us, that is, life's brevity, its insecurity, so that in the wisdom of this knowledge we may turn our hearts to things most worthy of the time that does remain.

If the first memorable words on the Atomic Age underscored our peril, the second, understandably enough, proposed retreat. Lewis Mumford advised that we treat nuclear weapons as "unconceived and inconceivable." As I do not recall the full context in which Mumford used this phrase, it might be unfair to saddle him with its surface implications. Yet its straightforward simplification epitomizes one important response to the atomic age. It was all a mistake. The power and possibilities nuclear energy makes available to man are too much. Once hubris asserts itself, nemesis is inevitable.

To this position there are three replies: it is irrelevant now; it was impossible then; and it is unseemly whenever. It is irrelevant now because history cannot be repealed; the point of no return was passed before Mumford's words were uttered. By now the realities of the atomic era lap around us in missiles, medicine, and power plants, as part of our daily life. It was impossible then, because had we left nuclear power untouched, the Nazis would not have. The basic point, however, is that this is no stance for man. Suppose any one of us had been given dictatorial power in 1940 to mark the nucleus off limits for mankind forever. Would he have done so? Should he have done so? Man wants to know, and he wants to enlarge the sphere of his autonomy, including control of nature. Being imbedded in his makeup, these drives will out; the fact that they involve risks will not deter their advance. In this sense the irreversible decisions were made neither on December 6, 1941, when the Metallurgical Project of the University of Chicago was authorized, nor in the summer of 1945, when the decision was made to drop the first bomb. The irreversible decision was the decision to create man.

A third notable word on man in the atomic age was spoken by Robert Hutchins. Appearing on the University of Chicago Roundtable of the Air on the Sunday following the Hiroshima blast, President Hutchins used the French philosopher Léon Bloy's phrase "the good news of damnation" to say, "It may be that the atomic bomb gives the good news of damnation; that it may frighten us into that Christian character and those righteous actions and those positive political steps necessary to the creation of a world society not a thousand or five hundred years hence, but now."

Seventeen years have passed since those words were spoken, and truth requires us to say that the hope they voiced was unfounded. It appears that man is not a creature easily frightened into virtue. For one thing, he can apparently get used to anything. "Total war," "the absolute weapon," "overkill"— how smoothly these words flow from our lips, how softly they fall on our scare-logged ears, how coolly we can now read Herman Kahn's guide to the playing of international Russian roulette. Live long enough under the sword of Damocles and eventually you ignore it.

The other flaw in the "news of damnation" theme lies in its exaggerated faith in the efficacy of negative motivation. Fear, we should never forget, has fascination; at least it is not dull. Moreover, its object is rarely inevitable. Consequently, fear alters behavior less than do desire or love, a point Thomas Chalmers saw clearly in his classic sermon on "The Expulsive Power of a New Affection." The moral seems to be that we shall not get the world society we need out of fear of what may happen in its absence. We shall get it when we want it.

The fourth observation takes the form of an image. In his study of the decision first to make the atomic bomb and then to drop it, Robert Bachelder likens nuclear weapons to an irritant grain in an oyster. Just as the oyster constructs a pearly coat to protect itself against its irritating intruder, so the human race is now engaged in trying to build up a coat to contain the colossal irritant nuclear weapons represent in its body politic.

This image of the oyster is suggestive in several ways. For one thing, the oyster cannot expel the sand grain. This symbolizes the fact that the world cannot get rid of nuclear weapons—cannot dismantle them through disarmament agreements, say. The only hope is to contain them, that is, to get them turned over, eventually, to an international police force. For, given the jungle atmosphere of international politics today, no nation is going to reduce its strength until there exists a supranational power to which it can look to safeguard its rights. Consequently, apart from some form of world government, disarmament is a mirage, and talk of it does no more than "give to airy nothing a local habitation and a name." Whether the nations will succeed in evolving the requisite world authority is an open question. If they do, it will in truth be the pearl of great price. "Great price" in a double sense: in its cost to us in imagination, effort, and the transcending of parochial loyalties and in its inestimable worth to us in assuring the continuance of human history.

Finally there is the simple truth of Albert Einstein's reminder that "the real problem is in the hearts of men." Left alone, missiles will, of course, do nothing; they will rest quietly on their launching pads. What needs to be controlled is us.

Men's minds, however, should be added to their hearts in Einstein's statement: it should read, "the real problem is in the hearts and minds of men." It would be wonderful if mankind could "go critical" in humaneness—if a chain reaction of charity could lead to a veritable explosion of global love. But this appears not to be a possibility. Instead, heart and head are going to have to work patiently and in complement as we seek to preserve this great and lovely world in which we have been given, thus far, to live.

How much influence the mind has upon the heart— reason has on virtue—is a moot question. But it is appropriate that, gathered as we are on a Sunday morning on a university campus, we reaffirm the fact that it has some. Facts do not give us our faith, but they certainly influence it; witness the numbers who are currently beguiled by certain facts of science into believing that mechanism, epiphenomenalism, and behaviorism outline man's true status in the universe. Mind meshes with heart on more proximate levels as well: witness the accepted distinction between self-interest (a heart-directed way of life) which is enlightened (intelligent) and that which is not (unintelligent).

It has become an axiom of political theory that nations cannot act contrary to what they conceive to be in their self-interest. But no task is more important than to keep pushing the intellectual question, "How far can we move in the direction of humane action before our self-interest is, in fact, compromised?

One specific item will illustrate my point. In his prepared statement to the press two days before Thanksgiving, President Kennedy let pass a small, yet in its way fine, opportunity to contribute to the international goodwill which is as vital to our interest as to the Soviets. Speaking on the state of the Cuban crisis, and with the eyes of the nation upon him through television, he said, "May I add this final thought in this week of Thanksgiving: there is much for which we can be grateful as we look back to where we stood only four weeks ago—the unity of this hemisphere, the support of our allies, and the calm determination of the American people."

Why not grateful also for the reasonableness of the Soviets during these weeks when the world swung low in its arc of danger? Grant that it was in the Soviets' self-interest to be conciliatory; the fact remains that not all nations have proved capable of acting in their own reasonable self-interest. Realism and appreciation are not contradictories. Mr. Kennedy had acted with great realism; for this he deserves our heartfelt thanks. It would have cost him little to crown this realism with generosity and appreciation to help ease the world's vicious circle of hate and guilt. Unilateral disarmament may be bad politics, but we have come to a sad time if our tit-for-tat world allows no room for occasional ventures in unilateral nobility.

We asked, "Has the atomic age thrown any light on man?" The answer is "Yes." It provides no insights which are absolutely new, but it brings into clearer relief some points we had sensed only dimly or had seen and forgotten. It underscores life's precariousness. Frail as a reed, crushable as a moth, man has become, to our knowledge, the riskiest venture in all creation. It clarifies the direction of human history, the thrust of this history toward knowledge and control which refuses to be halted by prospects of danger, however great. It reveals the inadequacy of negative motivation. It previsions the possibility of man's collective life, the possibility of a genuine world order which has become infinitely relevant while remaining infinitely problematical. Finally, it shows us where the human problem lies, how deeply inward that problem is, how radically free man is to do with his gigantic options what he will, and how mind and heart will mesh in every decision he makes.

Let me close with these lines from Meister Ekhart: "There is no stopping place in this life—no, nor was there ever one for any man, no matter how far along his way he'd gone. This above all, then, be ready at all times for the gifts of God, and always for new ones."

3

THE LANDSCAPE
OF THE SPIRIT

The Lost Dimension and the Age of Longing

By Sidney E. Mead
University of Iowa

It is good now and then to try to take our bearings as we sail through, or drift with, the oceanic currents of the universe. For, as Abraham Lincoln said, "If we could first know where we are and whither we are tending, we could better judge what to do and how to do it."

But to know where we are and whither tending religiously is not easy. Even a modicum of confidence that we are following a charted course to some destination other than dusty death rests upon an unstable foundation of knowledge, faith, and desire. Therefore, in speaking of where I think many of us are today, all I can hope to do is sketch an impressionistic mood picture concocted of some sound history, hunches, and sheer feeling.

In sketching such a picture I am quite aware that we today, as unique individuals and heirs of all the diversity provided by the attics of the ages, live mentally and spiritually in different worlds. My impression of our present religious state may not be yours. So be it. I have no desire to make converts and trust you have none either. But where are we?

Max Weber once characterized the movement of history during the past several centuries as "the progressive disenchantment of the world." More recently a historian characterized the history of the past two centuries as the story "of ultimate solutions gone sour." Both leave the impression that there has been a linear movement along a chronological line from "faith" to "doubt." The impression is wrong. History is not that simple, except to the simpleminded.

I have a friend—a professor and historian—who has published many volumes on the history of Christianity from his point of view. To me he appears to live in a stable belief-world in which the Scriptures provide a source of certain knowledge about man's past, present, and future and a definite set of standards for judging the meaning of events and the values to be sought. He lives in a world different from the one I inhabit. But he lives, and he is productive, and he seems to be as contented as the lot of man permits. He "believes" in the traditional sense.

At the other end of the spectrum, I know, and you know (perhaps from personal experience), people who live in what has been called "the existential vacuum." Such people, being human, are not guided by instincts. Their drift with the intellectual Gulf Stream of Western civilization has carried them far away from traditional religious beliefs. Of such a person an eminent psychiatrist has said, "No instinct tells him what he has to do, and no tradition tells him what he ought to do; soon he will not know what he wants to do. More and more he will be governed by what others want (and tell) him to do." This describes the "lonely crowd" of David Riesman's "other-directed people."

These extremes of belief and unbelief are contemporary. The two poles do not represent a chronological movement as is often supposed. But by and large we intellectuals are toward the belief-vacuum end of the continuum. Perhaps most vocal are those for whom an exhibitionist lack of belief is the hallmark of sophistication. So they pluck the strings of their rebellion against the "faith of our fathers" and chant their cleverness in ferreting out the absurdities of religion. It is better that they should be thus than apathetic.

But for others the kill has been made—the enemy slain. For them the old religious orthodoxy is dead, and to them it seems silly to continue to beat a corpse. As the lust of the hunt and the battle has cooled, reflectively they examine the dead face of religious belief and it "seems no longer that of an enemy." Perhaps their mood is close to that of Archy—Don Marquis' famous cockroach—as he saw the moth fly into the flame and become "a small unsightly cinder":

> i wish
> there was something i wanted
> as badly as he wanted to fry himself.

It is the mood of those who would like to believe but have discovered that they cannot believe, at least on the terms commonly offered them. They realize now that "believing" is not something one can, by taking thought, turn on or off. It is not a matter of simple choice, but something that flows to one through subtle channels that Christians know as "grace."

"So I won't believe," some say. But it is not as simple as that either. For apparently if one is to live at all, it is not optional whether he will believe in something or not. "Where there is no vision the people perish," wrote the ancient author of Proverbs. And two psychiatrists who watched their fellow prisoners live and die in the concentration camps have said about the same thing respecting individuals. Wrote one, "the vast majority of the thousands of prisoners who died at Buchenwald each year died soon. They simply died of exhaustion, both physical and psychological, due to a loss of desire to live." To this the other adds, "The prisoner who had lost faith in the future—his future—was doomed. With his loss of belief in the future, he also lost his spiritual hold; he let himself decline and become subject to mental and physical decay." But, believe what?

The difficulty many people have with much of orthodoxy is the seeming insistence of its representatives that "you must believe this, and you must believe it this way." It is for this reason that people in churches are often afraid to express their doubts and sometimes feel guilty for having them. It was encouraging to note in yesterday's *News* that today and tomorrow across the Midway a conference of Protestant, Roman Catholic, and Jewish laymen are beginning their discussion of "The Relevance of Faith in Modern Man" with a frank recognition that doubt of the beliefs and practices of his church often betokens the dawn of the member's real faith in God.

I am speaking to those people for whom traditional orthodoxy, as they have known it, is dead and who know that for them it is dead. At most, with Matthew Arnold on Dover Beach, they hear "Its melancholy, long, withdrawing roar." They poignantly stare at the dead face of the old religious belief and sense within themselves a lost dimension—a vacuum to be filled, a longing. A longing for what?

Perhaps few would say it as I say it. They are longing for a "church," almost, not quite, in the traditional sense.

We Americans are the heirs of all the ages, of every land, of every people. But most of the basic motifs of our culture were launched on that "sea of faith" that "was once, too, at the full." It has been said that a culture is the tangible form of religious belief and that the religion of our culture is—or was—the Christian religion. For centuries—say, from the fourth to the eighteenth—the great majority of our Western ancestors lived and moved and had their being in the context of the Christian drama. It was a wonderful myth of the life of Everyman and of Mankind.

The story of creation, redemption, and judgment enabled the average man to understand universal experience, "and it consoled him . . . to realize that his own life, however barren and limited . . . was but a concrete exemplification of the experience which God had decreed for all the generations of men." He was, as Emerson, held down to his place by the weight of the universe. He knew that at the end there would be a day of reckoning when infallible judgment, cutting through the moral and spiritual ambiguities known to man, would separate the evil from the good and allot to each his just reward. Then would the great judge stoop from above and wipe the tears from the tired eyes of the humblest person when he put earth's burdens down. He knew what human life was, for he was once born of a woman— "O little town of Bethlehem"—lived as a man among men, "was crucified dead, and buried." But "the third day he rose again from the dead," and that is why the great hallelujah chorus reverberates down through the ages.

Sadly it must be said that somewhere along the line for many people the curtain went down on that drama and that neither curtain nor God have risen again. Friedrich Nietzsche's mad man still rushes about in our market places crying, "I seek God! Where is God gone? I mean to tell you! We have killed him—you and I! God is dead!"

"Our God is dead!" The line has become so common that even timid clergymen now use it in an attempt to be "honest to God." Meanwhile, an increasing number of people who believe well enough that *that* God is dead, say it with the sad observation expressed by one of Arthur Koestler's characters, "Each time a god dies there is trouble in history."

But why did our God die? Did we kill him? If we did, I think it was unintentional deicide, committed while we thought we were but obeying His command to go forth and gain dominion over all other created things.

So we may point to that vast, vague area in our history that we call "the rise of science." Concurrently, men of faith began to realize that as they marched to fulfill this promise their universe was changing into an immense machine that ran with inexorable precision and without concern for man. The subtle alchemy of human experience was changing God the father of the Lord Jesus Christ with whom we were fellow-heirs into an engineer mechanic who had designed and built the machine, but now was about as remote as those semimythical monsters who in the flat Olympus of Detroit design our automobiles.

A chill settled over the Christian world as God seemed to be fading away like Alice's Cheshire cat, leaving among a residue of the intellectually invincible a disembodied and sentimental grin. "It was," as Carl Becker put it, "as if a rumor . . . had at last become too insistent to be longer disregarded: the rumor that God, having departed secretly in the night, was about to cross the frontiers of the known world and leave mankind in the lurch." For many this meant what Bertrand Russell suggested: "that man is the product of causes which had no prevision of the end they were achieving; that his origin, his growth, his hopes and fears, his loves and his beliefs, are but the outcome of accidental collocations of atoms . . . that the whole temple of man's achievement must inevitably be buried beneath the debris of a universe in ruins."

For the first time in Christendom people were confronted with the question "Are you living in a world ruled by a beneficent mind, or in a world ruled by an indifferent force?" But what really shocked them was that when they finally became self-consciously aware of the question, they had already accepted the latter answer. One of their spokesmen toward the end of the nineteenth century exclaimed that he "could not agree . . . that the 'new faith' constituted a desirable substitute for 'the waning splendour of the old.'" There is, he continued, an "appalling contrast between the hallowed glory of that creed which once was mine, and the lonely mystery of existence as now I find it." Such men *felt* "the lost dimension."

What was the "new faith" of which this scientist spoke? It was faith in man. But this is no simple matter. It has been persuasively argued that as the eighteenth-century philosophers dismantled the celestial heaven they rebuilt it on earth of earthly materials. Rejecting salvation mediated through the one who was "truly man and truly God," they postulated salvation through the efforts of successive generations of men. Living on in posterity took the place of an immortality in heaven as a sustaining belief. Robespierre, one of the leaders of the French Revolution, addressed a prayer to the new-model god: "O posterity, sweet and tender hope of humanity, thou are not a stranger to us; it is for thee that we brave all the blows of tyranny; it is thy happiness which is the price of our painful struggles; often discouraged by the obstacles that surround us, we feel the need of thy consolations; it is to thee that we confide the task of completing our labors, and the destiny of all unborn generations! . . . Make haste, O posterity, to bring to pass the hour of equality, of justice, of happiness." Thereafter down through the nineteenth century—indeed, down to the present for many people— the hope for one's future and hence the significance of one's life, was found in identification with a movement that was likely to endure in history. So Abraham Lincoln at Gettysburg said, "The world will little note, nor long remember what we say here, but it can never forget what they did here."

Men holding this belief could be as naively rapturous about the bright future of man on earth as the writer of the Book of Revelation was about the New Jerusalem where death would have no dominion and where there would be no night. Listen to Winwood Reade, writing in 1872:

> *The beautiful legend will come true; . . . Earth, which is now a purgatory, will be made a paradise, . . . by the efforts of man himself. . . . Hunger and starvation will then be unknown. . . . Governments will be conducted with the quietude and regularity of club committees. The interest which is now felt in politics will be transferred to science. . . . Poetry and the fine arts will take that place in the heart which religion now holds. . . . Not only will Man subdue the forces of evil that are without; he will also subdue those that are within. . . . A time will come when Science will transform [men's bodies] . . . Disease will be extirpated; the causes of decay will be removed; immortality will be invented. . . . [and] Man then will be perfect; . . . he will therefore be what the vulgar worship as a god.*

That, also, was a beautiful faith—a faith by which thousands of enlightened people lived and did great deeds, creating an era when even "wise men hoped" and believed in progress.

But sadly it must be said that God, incarnate in mankind and consequently immortal only as posterity is immortal—that god also died in 1945, when a pigmy bomb left a mushroom-shaped cloud over a Japanese city. What men like Winwood Reade hailed as the god who would transform men's lives and institutions and invent immortality for all had shown another face. The potential producer of all good was now seen as the potential producer of universal death by flame and radiation, or by slow starvation because of overpopulation, or by sheer pollution of the earth's surface. Man may go out with a big bang, or perhaps he will merely whimper as he suffocates in his own garbage. The Psalmist might say, "God gave them their request; but sent leanness into their soul." Or, "he gave them what they asked, but sent a wasting disease among them."

Slowly it seems to be dawning upon those people who placed their faith and found meaning for their lives in progress through posterity that there may be no "ever after" for mankind to live happily in. There may be no future. Posterity, worshiped as a god, may be even more vulnerable than the old Christian God because we can kill him as easily as we can "overkill" mankind.

There are, then, two aspects of the "lost dimension"—the loss of the ability to believe in the traditional Christian sense and the loss of ability to assure ourselves that a posterity is a sure thing. For many people, god the latter is as dead as god the former. It is because the faith in man's future which the eighteenth century taught us to substitute for faith in the Christian God has also collapsed that this becomes *The Age of Longing*, the title of Arthur Koestler's novel of 1951.

Longing for what? Longing for faith, for belief, for a meaning to one's life, and the work one does, for the ability to see something more than "a tale told by an idiot, signifying nothing" in the daily chores one has to do in order to live.

Of course this does not strike everyone at the same time or in the same way. Remember my friend who lives, and lives well, in the old Christian world. And I, as you, know technical intellectuals who still live, apparently quite happily, in the world of Winwood Reade. Others seem to be gifted with the capacity to earn enough in our affluent society to keep up with all the Joneses, all without any apparent concern about the family gods. Of course sometimes we eventually learn that as they gravitated toward the couch or into an expensive slumber room they had been living lives of "quiet desperation"—as Henry David Thoreau thought was the fate of most of his friends in staid old Concord. The people of Koestler's novel are these "dispossessed of faith; the physically or spiritually homeless." The burden of their anguish is, "Let me believe in something."

What I have given is the description of a mood—not universal, of course, but widely prevalent among sensitive people. These people cannot give themselves either to faith in the tradi-

tional sense or to the rich spontaneous faith in man and progress. Therefore it is not to be supposed, as some preachers seem
to suppose today, that ridiculing and undermining the belief in
man will restore the old kind of faith in God. But, on the other
hand, neither can it be supposed—as other preachers appear to
do—that undermining faith in the Christian God, where it still
exists, and ridiculing traditional Christian beliefs and practices
will restore the lost faith in man's future. A plague on both these
houses!

The people I have in mind seek religious faith.
Whether they would call it that or not does not matter. Their
mood, to repeat, is akin to that of Emerson's soldier who, after
the battle, realizes that the life he had to take cannot ever be
recalled—that an enemy once dead is no longer an enemy—that
the space he, or it, occupied may now be a fearful vacuum. It is
to these people that a church ought to speak—must speak if it
is to be more than a congenial company of irrelevant people.
What is to be said?

At this point, having tied the religious situation into
a desperately complex and hard knot, I wish that like some hardy
true believers I could pronounce it Gordian and cut it apart with
one deft stroke of the "Sword of the Spirit," the Word of God.
But already, it seems to me, too many preachers who do not even
understand the question these people of the age of longing are
asking are blithely telling them that "Jesus is the answer."

I cannot be that definite. I can only make a suggestion
through the use of figures. There is the figure of "the god behind
the gods." The tribes of men forget that human life is a pilgrimage and make comfortable camps beside lakes and pools of
truth from which they drink the water of life that sustains them
in their particularity. But, Thoreau once said, when a tribe's lake
or pool of truth dries up—as all lakes and pools must do—then
they must "gird up their loins once more, and continue their
pilgrimage toward its fountainhead." Some, of course, will resist
moving on and prefer to become fossilized in the drying mud of
the old pool. But those who do move toward the living stream
might well take as their slogan, "God is dead. God alone is
immortal!"

Then there is the figure of the Church. If the Church be these people on their pilgrimage toward the fountainhead of life, then the essence of that Church is to be found in the congenial relationship between these good companions. For God, 'tis said, is love. To find other people who are congenial company on the pilgrimage is to know the presence of that elemental love that is the creative ground of all human *being*.

So I can summarize what I have tried to say in words taken from J. Robert Oppenheimer: "this, as I see it, is the condition of man; and in this condition we can help, because we can love one another." I hope you can see what he meant, and I mean.

What You Worship as Unknown

By Lloyd J. Averill
Kalamazoo College

"The world of the Bible is not so different from our own contemporary world as we might think at first."

Many times we have heard that sentence, or its equivalent, in a sermon. Contrary to popular myth, preachers are acutely aware of the distance between the first century and the twentieth century. And there is fairly reliable evidence that this historical hiatus has not escaped the notice of those to whom preachers regularly preach. The minister who insists on centering his sermons in biblical proclamation is likely to be treated by some in his congregation with the same affectionate indulgence one reserves for potty old maid relatives who collect antique antimacassars.

So, partly in self-defense, the preacher speaks his sentence about the world of the Bible not being so different from our own contemporary world as we might think at first, and he follows that sentence with a valiant attempt to establish the points of contact between those two worlds. If, sometimes in desperate ingenuity, he comes up with interpretations which bear little resemblance to actual biblical history and little relevance to our own, he should at least be given credit for struggling with a difficult problem.

Now I have no intention of sailing under false colors in this matter. I am myself a biblical Christian—or at least I profess to be. I am myself convinced that sense can best be made of life from within those apprehensions of God and the world, ourselves and our fellows, which emerge out of the Christian revelation. And I am under no illusion about the difficulties which face one who believes that. Of course, there is a vast historical chasm separating the first century from the present century, although it is worth noting that the differences are not always where we expect to find them. Superficially, we may be tempted to contrast the credulity of the first century with the scientific knowledge of the twentieth, but that is sheer poppycock and pretentiousness. Whatever we may prefer to think, it is a fact that credulity did not suddenly disappear when the age of science was ushered in with Galileo's telescope and Anton van Leeuwenhoek's 247 microscopes. Modern men, as George Hedley has reminded us, have not ceased to be superstitious; they have simply adapted the old superstitions to their new situation. So we no longer believe in the efficacy of fertility rites, nor do we find credible the ancient myths which recounted the exploits of divine heroes. Instead we believe in the magic of the libido and the myth of the superior race.

We may be tempted to contrast the cruelty of the first century with the tenderness of the twentieth, but that is simply evidence of our blunted sensibilities. Today crucifixion has given way to the gas oven, and the stoning of the Christian Stephen by an unruly first-century mob seems almost humanitarian beside the bombing of Hiroshima and Nagasaki.

Still it is true that the differences between our own time and biblical times are real and important. One of the most striking and serious differences is to be found in an intriguing incident recorded in the Book of Acts. Paul of Tarsus, after a walk through the city of Athens, addressed a group of Greek philosophers with these words: "Men of Athens, in all things I perceive that you are very religious. For as I passed along, and observed the objects of your worship, I found also an altar with this inscription: To an unknown God." What Paul said in Athens he could have said with equal point in Ephesus or Corinth, in Rome or Jerusalem. Everywhere in the ancient world the fateful reality of the gods was felt. Indeed the power of the gods was so tangible to men that the Athenians feared to risk the wrath even of obscure gods whose names they chanced not to know, and so as a kind of insurance against divine displeasure, they erected an altar "to an unknown god" and trusted that each anonymous deity would think it meant for him.

Then certainly in this we live in a vastly different time. Simply listen to those whom we have chosen to speak for us. Friedrich Nietzsche, for one.

> *God is dead. God remains dead. And we have killed him. . . . Is not the greatness of this deed too great for us? Must not we ourselves become gods simply to seem worthy of it? There has never been a greater deed; and whoever will be born after us— for the sake of this deed he will be part of a higher history than all history hitherto.*

Sigmund Freud, for another.

> *First of all, we know that God is a father-substitute, or, more correctly, an exalted father, or yet again, a representation of the father as seen and met with in childhood—as the individual sees him in his own childhood and as mankind saw him in the prehistoric times in the father of the primal horde. Later on the life of the individual acquired a different, a less exalted impression of him, but the childish image of him was preserved and it united with the inherited memory-traces of the primal father to form the idea of God.*

And Jean-Paul Sartre, for still another.

> *Existentialism is nothing else than an attempt to draw all the consequences of a coherent atheistic position. . . . Existentialism isn't so atheistic that it wears itself out showing that God doesn't exist. Rather, it declares that even if God did exist, that would change nothing. There you've got our point of view. Not that we believe that God exists, but we think that the problem of his existence is not the issue.*

Or, if Nietzsche is too violent, and if Freud and Sartre are too controversial, then the gentle and wistful Albert Camus.

> *The certainty of a God giving a meaning to life far surpasses in attractiveness the ability to behave badly with impunity. The choice would not be hard to make. But there is no choice, and that is where the bitterness comes in.*

Or if it is a scientific spokesman we must have in this age of science, then Julian Huxley.

> *For my own part, the sense of spiritual relief which comes from rejecting the idea of God as a supernatural being is enormous. I see no other way of bridging the gap between the religious and the scientific approach to reality. But if this rejection is once accomplished, the abyss has disappeared in the twinkling of an eye, and yet all the vital realities of both sides are preserved.*

And the impact of these voices upon the present student generation is summed up in these words written not long ago by a graduate student of philosophy at Harvard.

> *I was attending . . . the annual conference of a graduate fellowship program sponsored by one of America's great educational foundations. One of the main requirements for appointment to these fellowships is a conviction that the study of religion, and especially of the Christian tradition, is a vitally important element of a liberal education. Ninety-five percent of the fellows are church members.*
>
> *After one of the meetings a random group of eight of us gathered for an evening of conversation. Before it was over, we found (to the surprise, I think, of all of us) that each of us was an atheist in the traditional sense of the term—we denied the existence of "the living God" of historic Christianity. . . . Twice more during the conference I participated in similar*

*discussions with altogether different groups. Each
time the result was the same.*

Not all men respond in the same way to the announcement of God's absence from the contemporary world.
Some, like Nietzsche and Freud and Huxley, are relieved at last
to be rid of what they regarded as an enslaving and antiquarian
notion. Others, like Sartre and Camus, are embarrassed and even
bitter at the discovery of a void at the heart of things. And still
others, like our young graduate student, are exhilarated at coming upon so serviceable a weapon with which to establish their
independence of an older tradition.

I am not for the moment interested in trying to demonstrate to one who no longer calls upon the name of God that
he has fallen into error. Indeed, I am quite convinced that the
existence of God cannot be demonstrated at all, if one means
by that fashioning so logically compelling an argument that anyone who exposes himself to it will end by falling upon his knees
in submission. What I am interested in trying to demonstrate is
that, even if our skeptical world stands somewhat in contrast to
the world of the Bible, that does not mean that the skeptical man
of the twentieth century represents a different breed of humanity
from the man of the first century. However much we may want to
ignore or reject the specific remedies which the Bible offers to our
condition, what we cannot do is divest ourselves of the condition
which the Bible discerns in us. That is what I am contending for
here. Then let me try now to say what that human condition is
as the Bible sensitively sets it forth. And as I do, remember that
it is not human nature in the abstract that is being described. It is
our own nature the Bible claims to know, and it is *our own* condition which I am here attempting to expose to view.

In one of his most vivid parables, Jesus spoke of a
man whose life was inhabited by an evil spirit. In due course the
spirit departed, leaving the spiritual life of the man unoccupied.
After a period of absence, that tenanting spirit said to himself,
"I will go back to the residence from which I came." And when
he returned, he found it uninhabited and inviting. So he enlisted
seven other spirits more evil than himself, and they all took up

residence in the man's life. And the last state of that man, said Jesus, was worse than the first.

The point of the parable is simple: no man's life stands empty. The void which is created in a man's or a woman's life when one set of meanings is outgrown or rejected is soon filled by another set of meanings, and there is no guarantee that the last state may not be worse than the first.

This, indeed, is just what religion is all about. Religion is only secondarily a matter of theological creeds and ritual observances and moral codes and churches. Primarily, religion is a matter of our meanings, and creed and ritual and code and church are only the servants, the tangible expressions, of the meanings which matter most. This is so often and so easily misunderstood that it is worth putting even more specifically: *Religion is the quest for that meaning which has power to give shape to experience, purpose to existence, and motivation and moral energy to the human enterprise.* Or, to say the same thing in another way, religion is the search for the answers to three questions: What is the meaning of life? What is the meaning of *my* life? Where shall I find the power to become what, in the light of that meaning, I can become?

No man's life stands empty, said Jesus, and the tragic record of our human search gives poignant and pointed emphasis to the words. Again and again it has proved true: when a man fails to find even a tentative or temporary meaning which can give shape to his experience, the consequence is inevitably psychosis or suicide. Life requires meaning to keep it from distortion or destruction. So for each of us, it is not a question whether we shall have a religion, but which religion we shall have. No man's life stands empty.

Then the world of the Bible is not so different from our own contemporary world as we might think at first. I am making *that* my own assertion now, and I submit that it takes little ingenuity to trace the connections. The sensitive observer of our twentieth-century scene will reach a conclusion about our modern culture which can be expressed in the same words which Paul of Tarsus addressed to the Athenians: "In all things I perceive that you Athenians are very religious. For as I passed among you, I observed the objects of your worship."

See this where you may not have thought to look for it. What is the preoccupying theme which runs through our popular books and magazines, which is portrayed in the theater and motion pictures, and which sets the pattern for much of our personal encounter? Surely it is our preoccupation with physical intimacy. To speak of that, as some do in roundly righteous terms, as pornography and sexual decadence is to miss the point. It is to miss the profound significance—the profound and desperate religious significance—of that preoccupation. Not long ago a novel appeared which, like many recent novels, seemed superficially to be just a sequence of bedroom scenes. The author of the novel suggested a deeper significance. He wrote that his book "is among other things an elegy upon the immemorial loneliness of man; a statement too about its causes (varied) and customary cure (someone charming to hold one's hand)."

May it not be true, then, that this preoccupation with physical passion is the vivid, though tragic, symbol of contemporary man's loss of meaning in an age when old meanings have been swept away? May it not be true that sexual experience is the refuge to which he flees in hope of filling the emptiness which must be filled if life is to be lived? Is it really surprising that he tries to find that personal communion out of which real meanings arise by a desperate drive toward physical closeness? One of the characters in a novel by George Simenon confirms what I am suggesting here. Speaking of his experience with his mistress he says, "For a few hours she gave me the sensation of infinity"; and of the response of the mistress herself he says, "her sexual excitement was a labored excitement. She clung to it as though to escape a void." No man's life stands empty.

Then I will not shrink from insisting that in many of us the pattern of our sexual preoccupation is a form of religious ritual, a part of our urgent search for some new god to replace the gods we have rejected. For the fact is that even an age which is proud of its professed atheism cannot get on without a god. It may, of course, get on without some particular god. What men have come to doubt in our own time is the existence of a superpersonal, a supernatural being. They have come to doubt, as our graduate student put it, "the living God of historic Christianity."

But that is only because they have found, at least temporarily, other objects for their trust. No man's life stands empty. Indeed, at bottom the question about God is the question about what it is in this vast existence that a man can finally trust. It is a strange fact of our human nature that we cannot really trust ourselves until we have found something to trust in the world beyond ourselves. Our growth from immaturity to maturity can be understood as the search for that which is trustworthy in the wider world. As children we sought to discover those elements within our limited environment which were dependable, which assured us that the world was not finally indifferent to us—our nurse, our mother, even our father if we cried long and loud enough. As we grew, this search for something to trust moved from unconscious need to conscious quest. As our world expands, becomes more complex, those nearer objects which we trusted as children appear limited, worthy of only a limited trust. Those persons and things which once were the boundaries of our world are now seen to be bounded themselves by a larger world. So we transfer our trust for a time to that which commands our attention, or that which stirs our imagination—education, science, technology, art, world government—only to discover that these too are limited and unsteady, bounded by destinies which stand beyond themselves.

So in full maturity what we come to ask is this: Is there finally in life anything worth trusting completely? Is there at the heart of things any assurance that the universe is not mere cold indifference? Is there ultimately anything in this vast and shifting world which is dependable, which will not betray me, which will stand though all else falter and fall?

The only real atheist is the man who says, "Nothing in life is worth my trust." And that, I suggest, is at best a temporary view for any of us. Normal existence has a way of requiring us to declare our loyalties. Whatever you find in life to which you are finally willing to commit your trust is your god. For each of us it is not a question whether we shall have a god, but which god we shall have. No man's life stands empty.

The world of the Bible is not so different from our own contemporary world as we might think at first. That does not make us all Christians without knowing it, but it does at least suggest that Christian faith is still an option for men and women who thought they had outgrown the need for it. The fact that we are incurably religious, that our lives are sometimes curiously set in a pattern of ritual where we would least expect to find it, that a thoroughgoing and consistent atheism is never really an option for us—these things at least ought to encourage in us an openness to the Christian word as a word spoken to our condition.

I cannot demonstrate the existence of the Christian God. I can only confess my own faith in the God and Father of our Lord Jesus Christ. I can only affirm that in place of the restless quest which drives us from one tentative faith to another, in Jesus Christ I have met the God who has Himself taken the initiative, who does not wait to be found but comes out in search of us. I can only affirm that in place of the compulsive search for a meaningful intimacy with life I have met, in Jesus Christ, the God who —incredibly—cared enough about human life to share it, and thus overcome the cosmic loneliness which often threatens to undo us. I can only affirm that in place of the disappointment which comes in the repeated discovery that we have put our trust in weak and empty things I have met, in Jesus Christ, the God whose defeat of death discloses his mastery over life.

When Helen Keller was a child, those who were responsible for her welfare decided that she ought to have religious instruction. Phillips Brooks, one of the best-known churchmen of the past century, was invited in to tell the Christian story to that child whose world was so terribly enclosed by blindness and deafness and dumbness. She placed her hands upon his face, for that was her only means of communication, and Phillips Brooks told her the story of Jesus Christ. When he had finished the child responded in excitement, "I knew him! I knew him! I didn't know his name, but I knew him." What the child had dimly apprehended, even through brutal handicap, Phillips Brooks had named with the Christian name.

If there is one who has wrestled in the deeps of his own being with an "unknown God," who has felt within his own experience, however dimly, the presence of a power and purpose not his own, and who would draw that presence into nearer focus, then my final word is for him. "What you therefore worship as unknown, this I proclaim to you."

The Word of the God Who Won't Talk

By Tom F. Driver
Union Theological Seminary

Today is Palm Sunday, but I am not going to preach a Palm Sunday sermon. Next Sunday is Easter, but I am not going to preach an Easter sermon either. Instead, I am going to preach about what comes in between Palm Sunday and Easter, namely, the Crucifixion. My text is Matthew 26:68: "Prophesy to us, you Christ. Who is it that struck you?"

Every age has its characteristic way of experiencing and describing religious doubt. In some ages, men have expressed religious doubt by denying the existence of God. Some people do that today, of course, but it is not the characteristic way our own age has of expressing its doubt.

What most people deny today is that there is any communication between God and man. "God may exist or not," they say. "Who cares? The point is that he has nothing to do with us." W. H. Auden has said that our times are characterized by the feeling that God is distant. Many men are willing to agree that God may be there, but they say that he is so remote that he is irrelevant. He has nothing to do with the world we inhabit, the thoughts we think, the emotions we feel, the life we live. I have an acquaintance who says, "God used to act in the affairs of men, he used to speak. That was in biblical times. But now he has withdrawn himself, he has put us on our own." Even the theologians today reinforce the feeling that God is distant. Many of them speak of God as what they call "the wholly Other." They talk about the "infinite abyss" which separates man from God. They divide the Creator from the creature. God is distant.

It is not a new feeling. "Thou didst hide thy face," wrote the Psalmist, "and I was troubled" (30:7). And Job asked, "When he hides his face, who then can behold him?" God may exist, but he is hidden somewhere. He is as remote as a distant star. In the space age, he is even more remote.

Nevertheless, people in our day continue to look for God. In spite of his distance, his silence in the great somewhere, or maybe just because of those things, they continue to try to search him out. They want to know what he is like. They want to know the mystery that surrounds him.

You find this search going on in the most unlikely places. In Tennessee Williams' works, for instance. One of the most garish and most impious plays of Williams, that study of perversion called *Suddenly Last Summer*, goes out of its way to describe a man's search for the nature of God. Sebastian Venables was what the headshrinkers call a sado-masochistic personality. He once went down to the beach to watch some baby turtles being hatched. Some of them came out of the eggs lying upon their backs, with no way to turn themselves over. Large buzzards came down and preyed upon these helpless baby turtles, picking at their soft, exposed undersides, until they killed and devoured them. "When Sebastian saw that," a character comments, "he believed that he had seen God." In other words, Sebastian Venables hunted in nature for an image of absolute, naked violence, and when he saw it he said his search for God was over. Says another character in the same play, "We take the alphabet blocks in the nursery and throw them around, hoping they will spell the name of God."

Take *Long Day's Journey into Night*. Edmund Tyrone, which is just another name for the playwright, Eugene O'Neill, tells of the time he lay aboard ship and for once in his life was happy. He had a vision. He says.

> *Like a saint's vision of beatitude. Like the veil of things as they seem drawn back by an unseen hand. ... For a second there is meaning! Then the hand lets*

*the veil fall and you are alone, lost in the fog again,
and you stumble on toward nowhere, for no good
reason!*[1]

"Oh, that I knew where I might find him!" cried Job. "I would lay my case before him and fill my mouth with arguments" (23:3–3). But the trouble with God is that he won't talk.

Why won't God talk? One might have had the same question when Jesus, he who is called the Christ, was led in front of his accusers at the trial before they put him to death. Here was, above all, the place to make the grand defense. He was a witness on the stand, and everyone is willing to listen to the accused. He might have made the greatest grandstand speech of history, the great oration that would sum up in concentrated form all that God had to say to man. But instead, he did not even properly defend himself. The high priest stood up and said, "Have you no answer to make? What is it that these men testify against you?" But Jesus was silent. Man may ask the questions. But God won't talk.

In a way, of course, God does talk. But his talking often seems to tell us even less than his silence.

He was silent for a few moments, then Jesus opened his mouth to speak. He said, "I tell you, hereafter you will see the Son of man seated at the right hand of Power and coming on the clouds of heaven." Now, what kind of talk is that?

If we speak to God, or to Jesus, who claims to speak for Him, we want plain answers. We want to ask the question "Who are you" and not be befuddled by the reply. We want to know "What are you going to do about the world" and not be put off by indirections. We want clarity and we want justice. We want to understand the things we don't understand, and we want the things that are wrong to be put right. Now, that's simple enough, and God's reply ought to be in that kind of language.

Instead, we get all kinds of runarounds. We get figurative, poetic statements about the son of man coming on the

[1] Reprinted by permission of Carlotta Monterey O'Neill and Yale University Press. Copyright © 1959 by Carlotta Monterey O'Neill.

clouds of heaven. We get the Bible, which is said to be the word of God and is full of contradictions, absurdities, and all kinds of outmoded ideas. The Bible is so obscure it makes modern poetry read like a primer. Or God speaks through the Church, which looks like either a broken-down organization or else a hypocritical one.

Mythology, ancient scripture, the Church. This kind of thing is as bad as no language at all, or perhaps it's worse. It seems to us like a smoke screen, some kind of deliberate intention to mix everything up. Why can't God declare himself without double-talk? Why won't he come across? The trouble with God is he won't level. He won't talk.

At this point, if we care at all, and we do, we strike back. When the language of communication breaks down but people still want to get through, communication flows into the muscles and the emotions and comes out as violence. Have you ever watched a child trying to say what it couldn't say? It grows angry, its muscles tense, face flushed, and it stamps the floor; if its frustration is not relieved, it will strike. As Billy Budd struck Claggart, it will lash out. Or as a violent lover, repulsed by his love, turns upon her to storm the barricade by force.

Even so, the crowd turned upon Jesus, who either gave them no answer to their questions or an answer they could not understand.

Then the high priest tore his robes and said, "He has uttered blasphemy. Why do we still need witnesses? You have now heard his blasphemy. What is your judgment?"

They answered, "He deserves death." Then they spat in his face and struck him. Some slapped him, saying, "Prophesy to us, you Christ. Who is it that struck you?" "Here! Look at me!" cry his tormentors. "Who do you think's talking to you now? Whose fist is this that's going in your face?" Force is applied instinctively, ironically, as the only language he would understand. It is the pathetic last resort of people who would make God talk.

You and I live in an age of blasphemy. Every insult that could be imagined has been hurled in the face of God. It was not only that certain bookish theorizers called him the opiate of the people, or that others called him an illusion and said that his worship depended on the castration complex. More recently we have had from England the angry young men and from California the priests of the beat generation. The angry ones have been angriest of all at God, shaking their fists at him and sneering at his very name. The so-called beat boys have been more subtle. They have embarked upon their own quest for salvation. Jack Kerouac himself said theirs was a religious quest. Their recipe: salvation by outrage. Dope, cultism of all kinds, furious sex— what is it but the eagerness to achieve the ultimate by some kind of unholy ritual? They are angry or fed up with the language of God, and they therefore attempt to communicate in their own way with the language of blasphemy.

Perhaps the great modern hero is Melville's Captain Ahab, who sailed the *Pequod* in quest of Moby Dick. His great words were blasphemous defiance, yet they cloaked a kind of worship. Said he to God:

> *I own thy speechless, placeless power. . . . Nor was it wrung from me; nor do I now drop these links. Thou canst consume; but I can then be ashes. Thou canst blind; but I can then grope . . . defyingly I worship thee!*

This is the language of those who struck the Christ and then cried, "Prophesy to us, you Christ. Who is it that struck you?" It is the deepest attempt of man to make himself heard, to get through to God, to get through to the God who does not talk our language.

What language does God talk? He talks the language of deeds rather than words. Or as I should say, his word is his deed. And the deed through which God speaks his word to us is the deed in which he receives upon himself the blows that we deliver when we cannot understand. The name for this is crucifixion.

The story of the smiting and scourging of Christ by the crowd is a forerunner of the humiliation and death which Christ suffered upon the cross. The death of Jesus is the final word which God speaks. As Paul puts it, "the word of the cross is the power of God."

What does this mean? It means that we cannot get through to God, nor he to us, until we realize that we inflict injury upon him, and that he does not reply with retaliation but with love.

Guenter Rutenborn's play *The Sign of Jonah* takes place in a courtroom in which various persons are on trial for their part in recent "crimes against humanity." It does not matter what the crimes are: gas chambers, gestapo methods of terrorism, atomic bombs on helpless cities, the bombing of a Jewish temple, discrimination against minorities—what have you. Ordinary people defend themselves, and all are able to show that they are able to show that they are not responsible for these things. After all, they had their lives to lead, their families to support, and they pretty much had to do as they were told. Besides, they have suffered as much as the next person, and there is no reason they should suffer more when they are only relatively guilty. Politics is then brought to trial in the person of an exotic queen, and she also is able to prove that what happened was not her fault. For she had to rule men as she found them. Whatever was done was done from necessity, because human nature is as it is.

When all have spoken, it becomes clear that no one can be sentenced for the atrocities. The queen then points out that the only one who could be held guilty, although they seem afraid to mention it, is God himself.

> *Who has made men so that one can rule them only by death and terror? Who has ordered the world so that kings must sin more than other people?*

She therefore proposes a sentence upon God. He should become a king. He should wear a crown; he "should be thrust from the highest honors into damnation of outrage and uncleanliness." The others join in this sentence. God should become a man, a wanderer on earth, "without rights, homeless, hungry, thirsty, terrified of death." He should suffer the pain of fatherhood and at last die, dishonored and ridiculed.

The court finds the sentence just, and the judge of the court goes out to carry the sentence to God. There is a long silence The lights dim, the characters on stage move their positions. In the silence, the audience becomes aware of the great irony upon which the Christian faith is built: that they who are guilty have found themselves innocent and have instead passed sentence upon their judge; but that the judge, who is innocent, will accept the sentence of the guilty and in so doing will take their guilt away from them. And still a further irony: He is not only willing to do this, he has already done it.

This is the word of love that God speaks to us. And it is the only word we are prepared to hear. It was Ahab himself who said, "Come in thy lowest form of love, and I will kneel and kiss thee." What Ahab did not know was that he had already come in that form and that he does so continuously. For he changes the very blows with which we strike him into his cross, which is his word of love.

The Unconstrained God

By *Lou H. Silberman*
Vanderbilt University

To the commentators of the past, as to the critical scholar of the present, the third chapter of Exodus has been an inexhaustible source of wisdom and a never-failing challenge to learning. For the rabbinic exegetes, Moses' faithful tending of Jethro's flock prepared him to become the faithful shepherd of the Israel yet in bondage. Their imagination caught fire from the bush that flamed, yet was not consumed, and they found, in the narrative of the journey behind the desert meanings that illumined their own times and lives.

For the critic, the riddle of the divine name, here revealed and concealed at one and the same time, has been the setting-off point for speculative journeys that are at times no less imaginative than their predecessors' homilies. Yet, like those who went before, they have not failed to bring back some bit of understanding unfamiliar and new, to make the text, unconsumed by the mind's flame, shed its light upon our way.

The poet knows that the subtle ambiguities of his lines both puzzle and delight; so though a thousand critics ply their trade and measure, make, and weigh his every word, around, among, amid them, the ultimate meaning which he himself may only faintly, if at all, discern will remain tantalizing for following generations to approach and wrest their meaning, the meaning of their days and ways from out his song.

86

These lines then we have read. These words have been peered at and puzzled over by a hundred generations. Have they disclosed all their meaning, so that like empty wine skins they wait only the new wine of our wisdom to fill them bursting with ultimate meaning? Or, as the medieval commentator said of Scripture's first words: "This verse cries out: But understand me!" And such a summons we cannot but heed.

Moses, straining at the tensions of his past, his Hebrew birth, his Egyptian upbringing, confused and perhaps filled with self-reproach for having sacrificed rank and honor to go out to his brethren, who seemed not to care for him, went out, say the commentators, again and again into the wilderness, the wastelands, drawn by the longing for wholeness and the half-prophetic certainty that somewhere among sand and rock and sky there was an answer. What he sought, he found. A wonder and a voice. But then the doubts rushed in. Who am I that I should go to Pharaoh and bring the children out of Egypt? "I will be with them," came the reply. How particularly unsatisfactory, Moses thought with Egyptian sophistication. If there is a voice, there is a someone who goes with the voice. This is an elementary axiom of dogmatic theology. All Egyptian gods have names and it is of great importance to know them. When you have the name you have the essence; and the essence set properly in a proposition like a gem in a mounting affords one a great deal of power. So Moses, with a proper introductory sentence to set the stage, concernedly said, "When *they* ask *me* 'What is *His* Name?' what shall *I* say to *them?*"

"Say this to the people of Israel, '*Eheyeh* has sent me to you.'" Then Moses suddenly knew he was not in the presence of any of the domesticated deities he had learned about in the academies of Amon-Re. The answer to his Egyptian question about the divine name was a divine evasion: I shall be there as I shall be there. I am there.

This, then, was the ancient God of whom he only faintly knew. A name whispered by his foster mother who was indeed his very mother. A name that was not really a name but a gesture, a shout, an acknowledgment. He is here. The father of his father's father, who too had fled into the wilderness, had waked and shudderingly cried, "In truth, He is in this place, this stony desolate waste, this place of fleeing, of exile, of shame, and I did not understand it." And centuries later in a beleaguered capital with siege mounds raised against the walls, another would say, "For God is here in these straits with us."

This was the unconstrained God, the God beyond the fetters of fashion, the chains of culture. No formula could contain Him; no proposition empty Him out. He was there as He would be there. Not in the pomp of procession, not summoned and bound by a magic name, but in the unpredictable and unexpected. Not from the stately cedar did He call, say the rabbis, but from the lowly thorn; not from Hermon's snowy peak, but from Sinai's crookback stone.

Is not this the word that speaks to us today? Though we would constrain God, bending Him to the preconceptions of our culture, He is with us as He will be, not as we would will Him be.

One teacher, leaning over his desk, was talking about the most dangerous of all parts of speech, the adjective. "Men," he said, "talk about a personal God. What do they mean? Not a God who is person, but a God who bears the adjective like a valet or a maid; one who is attached to me, to my person, for I am the center, not He."

Here then is a god whose name I know. My own little god whose task it is to perform convenient miracles for me and mine. A genie of the lamp who when I call must answer, "Yes, Master!" if I know the formula and use it aright, if I manipulate the words, health, wealth, position, fame, and mine from him. What a godlet shuffling along in the triumphal procession of me. He is the deity of the sundial that must admit, "I mark the sunny hours." But no god he of whom with voice weighed and broken with sorrow I can say in ancient words, "Blessed is the Righteous Judge," to mark my recognition of the mystery of His presence. No god of whom I can proclaim in the mist of my uncomprehending ignorance, "He is here." Nor of whom I would declare in the wilderness of my sorrow, in the desert of my despair, "Thou art the very heart of my joy!"

No! The God who encountered Moses behind the wilderness, who said of Himself, "I who am with them in this sorrow will be with them in every strait"—such a God cannot be cajoled or threatened as the ancient Egyptians and their contemporary counterparts scold their recalcitrant deities. He is met in the midst of life in all of its fullness, in the tension, the paradox of existence that lets one man proclaim, "Blessed be He who did not let His world lack anything," and another meditate,

> My God, Thou has made me hunger
>   and naked forsaken me;
> Set me in the darkmost night;
>   taught me Thy power and might.
> Though Thou burn me in fire
>   I shall but love Thee more
>   and find my joy in Thee.[1]

"I shall be there in thy life as I shall be there." This must we needs know. If then He will not be my personal God, perhaps He can be institutionalized. What is needed is not a name to manipulate, but a label nicely marked, a god ticketed and on display—"cribbed, cabined" and defined, a deity whose task it is to nod vigorously in assent to every proposal made to the greater glory of the institution and to frown fiercely at all who dare to question its divine right. Or more sophisticated than this, what is needed is the tamed god of the system, goose-stepping to the dialetical drill master's command.

While it is a great comfort to know that God is in pocket, there are moments when questions wake us in the night. What if He has escaped the net of our words, has fled the prison of our propositions, so that the god we proclaim is a mask covering the emptiness, the nakedness of our faithless faith?

It is not that we are joined together for naught, but that our union must be in humbleness of heart and soul and strength. It is not that we must condemn the wonder of the human mind as it throws its arches across the stream of mystery, but that we must remember that a part of that wonder is its restlessness. "Verweile doch du bist so schön," the acceptance of

[1] *The Language of Faith: Selected Jewish Prayers*, ed. Nahum N. Glatzer (New York: Schocken Books, 1947), p. 58.

any moment as ultimate, was to deliver Faust into Mephistoph-eles' waiting claw. The arrogance of contentment with any word we say as final—the word that seizes hold of God to bind Him grinding to the mill of our institution of our thought—drives Him from us. "I and the proud man cannot dwell in the same world" was the word the rabbis heard from the Presence of God.

I will be there not because the towers gleam or the thought is subtle but as I will be there among those who gather and serve in truth.

Perhaps then the fault lies in our having provided Him with too limited a stage. Give Him more scope; give Him history, the sweep of time, the spread of space, and He will play the role we have written. What is the script He is to follow, the lines He is to read? Not for us Voltaire's sardonic remark, "God is always on the side of the heaviest battalions." Ours is a more respectable God. Yet the cynical realism of such a quip is far less offensive—though equally untrue—than our present piety which proclaims that He is the public sponsor of the power politics of the nice people with good intentions. No Peter of Amiens, no Bernard of Clairvaux summoned a crusade with "Deus vult" with more assurance than some of our contemporary statesmen who are able to discern with a theological nicety (that would have amazed the Doctor Subtilissimus) which intercontinental bal-listic missile bears the divine seal of approval. Our modern "Sons of Light" are not only fully aware of the evil designs (and such they are) of the "Children of Darkness," but they are as well superbly confident of their own election. They have forgotten that Amos at Beth-El may have displayed the sins of Tyre, Damascus, Edom, and the rest in all their horror, but it was God's word "concerning the three sins of Israel, yea, the four" that was the focus and crux of his message. Though it was the God of Israel who spoke, it was not Israel's private, petted, and petty deity but the sovereign of nations making Himself known in judgment on kingdoms, demanding most from those whom He knew most intimately.

Or were we to echo in contemporary terms Isaiah's "Ah, Assyria, the rod of my anger the staff of my fury," would we really mean it? Do we indeed seek a Lord of history or only a defender of our civilization, a captain of our host? *Eheyeh asher Eheyeh.* I will be there in nations' rise and fall, in empires' might and toppling, as I will be there.

Is God then never to be found? Does He forever hide himself, so that we may never know Him? So long as we demand that He be with us on our terms—personal, institutional, national —so long as we would add Him to our collection of things to move and manipulate, to make him ours, we shall not find Him. But when in trust we turn to become and ever be His, then does He say, "Eheyeh," "I am here"; then does He become my God, encountering me in the wholeness of existence; then does His presence shine over our gathering and our pondering; then does the pattern of men and nations show forth His command and His demand. When we thus ask, "What is His name?" Not in cleverness nor pride but in enduring trust, the answer comes not in oracular words but in the thrust of existence, in the strain of life. Amid the light and the shadow, in the commingling of joy and pain, in the taste of gall and honey, we shall know the most secret name: *Eheyeh asher Eheyeh.* "I shall be there as I shall be there." *Eheyeh.* "I am there."

G—O—D

By William Graham Cole
Lake Forest College

When William Stubbs was Bishop of Oxford, he was asked by a young curate what to preach about. "Preach about God," the Bishop answered, "and preach about twenty minutes." However admirable the advice may seem (especially the latter part), it has become increasingly difficult for any honest man to preach about God, progressively so in every century since the Enlightenment.

I heard a delightful story recently about Titov, the first Russian cosmonaut. Back from his pioneering venture into outer space, he was granted a private audience with Premier Khrushchev, who asked him whether he had seen anybody out there. "Yes," said Titov, "I did. There is in fact a God." "I knew that already," said Khrushchev, "but please don't tell anyone." Later, the patriarch of the Russian Orthodox Church asked the cosmonaut if he had seen anybody out there. "No," said Titov, "there is no God." "I knew that already," said the patriarch, "but please don't tell anyone."

The story is significant for its suggestion that the official atheist believes in God and that the official high priest is an atheist. It is illustrative of the confusion that has spread among us for the last several centuries, a confusion which clusters around those three charged letters of the alphabet: G—O—D. That combination of symbols, or its equivalent in other languages, either spoken or written, will provoke the most diverse responses,

ranging from awesome reverence to wrathful scorn. Curiously it
is rare for either polar protagonist to ask or to answer the question
of what the letters really mean. Is it the *word* that matters? Is the
symbol itself sacred or profane as the case may be, or is it the
reality to which it points or from which it distracts that is important? At least this much service has been done us by one school of
contemporary philosophers. They have pointed out to us that
there is a difference between actual *things* and the names we
choose to call those things. When Adam and Eve were in process
of naming the various animals as they passed in review, Eve said
of one, "Let's call that a tiger." "Why a tiger?" asked Adam.
"I don't know," said Eve. "It just looks like a tiger!" All of which
simply reminds us that all words and names have something
about them that is arbitrary, as the nominalists insisted some
centuries ago.

So let us leave off arguing with one another about
three letters rather arbitrarily arranged and try if we can to talk
about what lies beyond them. Surely, this is what Bishop Stubbs
really meant. Men—that is to say, you and I—are creatures who
are concerned about values. We regard some things in life as
desirable, to be sought out, collected, cultivated, encouraged, and
strengthened. Others we want to avoid, weaken, downgrade,
perhaps even destroy. The former we call "good"; we value such
persons, objects, ideas, and activities. The latter we call "bad"; we
do not value such people, things, and deeds. Sometimes our
judgments in these matters are arbitrary and irrational, thinly
concealing our own vain and selfish thoughts and wishes, as both
Marx and Freud showed us. But at our best we seek to be rational
instead of rationalizing, producing ideas instead of ideologies. In
any case, we cannot avoid being concerned about values. Even
Freud and Marx had values.

Now there are those among us who want us to believe
that one value is as good as another, that it is impossible for anybody to make any distinctions or to arrange any sort of hierarchy.
These people are called "relativists," and right now they are very
much in fashion. They have made everyone suspicious of all
absolutes. There are, they say, no absolutes—except for the absolute that there are no absolutes. But let that pass for the moment,

and say that one end of a spectrum is represented by a viewpoint which holds that values are many and that no significant distinctions can be made among them. Call these people "polytheists," without in any way being critical or superior. At the other end of the spectrum are those whom we can label, again without praise or blame, as "monotheists." They believe that there is only one overarching, supreme Value—spelled with a capital "V." Here is to be found a great variety of human beings. By no means do all of them believe in G—O—D. Many Marxists in this category insist loudly that they are atheists, as do numerous orthodox Freudians and certain highly fashionable Existentialists. Some superpatriotic groups proclaim piously their faith in the Deity, but *their* monotheistic devotion proves, in fact, to be rather to a narrowly conceived political philosophy. This is perhaps the true hallmark of the monotheist; it is not so much that he says that there is only one supreme Value as that he proves to be the sole possessor, interpreter, and priest of that Value—he and his church or party or society, whatever the case may be. Many of my friends in biblical scholarship would insist at this point that such are not *true* monotheists but only the successors of Satan, who was rather a monomaniac, seeking to place himself on the throne of the cosmos. The genuine monotheist, according to the Bible, always knows that the supreme Value far transcends and surpasses him as an individual. "My thoughts are not your thoughts, neither are your ways my ways," says Yahweh, "for as the heaven is high above the Earth, so are my ways higher than your ways and my thoughts above your thoughts." The genuine monotheist knows himself to be judged, weighed in the balance, and found wanting by the supreme Value. The pseudomonotheist is the spokesman, the high priest, the sanctified Messiah who is commended to purge the earth of the wicked and the unenlightened.

You and I can pass many a pleasant hour together discussing or debating whether there is in fact—in heaven or anywhere else—such a being as is described or suggested by the letters G—O—D. We can carry on such a discussion or debate without either of us being in the least affected or changed. But when we begin to explore and to challenge each other's values, not the abstract ideas to which we may give lip service, but the actual motives which direct our daily lives, then we are met in combat, in what William Blake called "War in Heaven." There is at least this much good in the heat of the present political campaign. We have stopped our polite fencing which concealed deep cleavages in political philosophy, and now we have at each other with a vengeance. The tipped foils are cast aside and broad-swords clash with stormy clangor. This is a religious struggle, a conflict of values; of different convictions about what matters most in our national life.

A lofty and lovely neutrality, so congenial to the professional intellectual, may be not only possible but even desirable in all sorts of questions which can be answered only in the mind. Is there a being called G—O—D? "I know not," responds the agnostic, casting a plague on the houses of both theist and atheist. But in a struggle over values—not in the abstract, protected, sanitized study—but in the arena where men live and work, love and die, there agnosticism becomes not only difficult but impossible. "Ah," but you say, "I cannot make a choice; I do not know." Unhappily for you and for all of us, not to choose is, in fact, to make a choice. Not to decide is already to have made a decision. To stand aloof is to cast a vote for the stronger side, whatever that may be. Stalin countered the suggestion that the Pope be invited to the peace table at the conclusion of World War II with the cynical question, "How many army divisions has he got?"

A vote for neutrality is a vote for the stronger divisions, as the Western democracies discovered to their sorrow in Manchuria, in Ethiopia, and in Spain. Skepticism is not viable as a way of life, however attractive and compelling it may be as a way of thought. This the ancient philosophers who took the name to themselves well understood. Aware that they did not know, and also aware that they had to act, they withdrew from the world and lived as hermits in order to minimize the evil effects of their inevitable and ignorant acts.

In the conflict of values which constitutes life, you may say that you cannot choose. Unfortunately, the world is such that you must choose—in what you do, in what you are, if not in what you believe or think. To live is to act, and to act is to choose, to decide, to testify to what it is one values. This is what the Bible means by those three loaded letters G—O—D—not some vague, distant being who may or may not exist somewhere. The Bible nowhere speculates about, discusses, or debates the existence of God, and for a very good reason. It is perfectly possible to affirm with one's mind the existence of a thoroughly orthodox deity and to affirm with one's life—in what is actually and concretely valued —that such a proper God is, in fact, dead. The Bible cares very little about what you think or believe, which is one reason for its low popularity rating in most educational institutions. The Bible insists on asking what you are, what you do, what you value with your deeds and with your dollars.

So let us understand one another. I want to follow Bishop Stubbs's advice to preach about twenty minutes about God, but not about some hypothetical being whose existence both you and I may doubt. I want to preach about our values, yours and mine, about what drives and directs us, about what the psychologists call our motivations, not because this is modern and fashionable, but because this is precisely what the Bible means by the word *God*. Either you value, you worship (which literally is to ascribe worth to), something which transcends yourself, including your family, your class, your nation, your race, your culture, even your religion, something which demands respect and reverence for all of life, however different and distinct it may be, or, as one book title has it, "Your God is too small." If those three letters still bother you, translate that to read "Your values are too limited." This is a virtue of the Bible which few sermons, including this one, possess; it is seldom abstract or theoretical. Nearly always it is very concrete. Its values are very clear. All men are brothers, the children of one father, and none can exploit or abuse another. He who would show his love for God can do so only by respecting, serving, yes, even loving, his neighbor. G—O—D. Those three letters are recognized as undefinable, meaningful only by analogy, by terms and experiences in the realm of human existence. Father, Judge, Lord, King—all these metaphors are used, but always *as* metaphors, never literally. The Old Testament even displays a severe reluctance to use the name *God* at all. Above all, the Bible stresses the term "love," and in the Old Covenant as well as in the new. "Where love is there God is." One verse finally says it straight out, but it is implied everywhere. "God *is* love."

So let us not argue with one another about a word. If you don't like these three particular letters, I shan't quarrel with you. I hope you know that there is such a thing as love and that it is, as Henry Drummond reminded audiences on both sides of the Atlantic a generation ago, "The greatest thing in the world." I hope also that you know that love is something you cannot confine only to those human beings whom you happen to approve or even like personally. It has the most devastating way of breaking down and leaping over every barrier men has ever tried to erect. In our own day it has annihilated distance and brought us all within a few hours' travel of each other and within seconds' communication. We have seen colonialism banished, and we watch with hope and fear as people everywhere seek what is their just due—simple human dignity and respect. Love—not mawkish sentimentality—but affirmation of others: "reverence for life" Schweitzer calls it. Love now confronts us with a challenge and a choice. Either we place ourselves on the side of those who seek to increase and to widen opportunities for all human beings everywhere, or we seek out of whatever motives to restrict and to confine privileges to those who already possess them. That is what is meant by the word *God*. It was so in ancient Israel and in the Palestine that knew Jesus. It is so today. To "preach about God," for however short or long a time, is to confront ourselves not with theological abstractions but with concrete decisions about values important to ourselves and to our world.

A young man who fancied himself as quite an orator attached himself to the band of disciples around St. Francis of Assisi. After a long apprenticeship, he was delighted when Francis asked for his company in a preaching mission in a particular city. All day long the youth joined the saint in visiting the poor and the sick, feeding the hungry, comforting the sad and the deprived. As the sun fell in the west, he asked Francis impatiently, "But when do we begin to preach?" to which Francis responded, "My son, what do you think we have been doing all day long?"

Ask and It Will Be Given You

By *Schubert M. Ogden*
Southern Methodist University

> *Jesus said to his disciples, "Ask, and it will be given
> you; seek, and you will find; knock, and it will be
> opened to you. For everyone who asks receives, and he
> who seeks finds, and to him who knocks it will be
> opened. What father among you, if his son asks for
> a fish, will give him a serpent; or if he asks for an egg,
> will give him a scorpion? If you then, who are evil,
> know how to give good gifts to your children, how
> much more will the heavenly Father give the Holy
> Spirit to those who ask him?"*
> —Luke 11:9–13

To the careful student of this text one thing about it immediately catches the eye. Except for some trivial details, it is an almost perfect parallel to another passage found in the Gospel according to Matthew (7:7–11).

I say almost perfect parallel because there is one important difference between the two passages which stands out all the more sharply because they are otherwise so much alike. In Matthew's version—which is certainly the older—the concluding sentence reads as follows: "If you then, who are evil, know how to give good gifts to your children, how much more will your Father who is in heaven give good things to those who ask him?" Luke, by contrast, replaces the words "good things"

98

with the words "the Holy Spirit," thus giving the whole text a rather different appearance than it has in Matthew. The content of the promise, "Ask, and it will be given you," is no longer defined by the wholly general term "good things" but is understood to be the quite specific gift by God of his own personal presence.

Except for this difference, of course, the Church would never have selected our text—even as late as it did—as a proper lesson for this Sunday, the Feast of Pentecost. But this suggests that a likely way to understand what the text would teach us is to reflect together on the significance of this difference. What's the point when the gift it promises simply for the asking is not the plural gift of "good things," but the singular gift of God's own Holy Spirit?

Perhaps if we can answer this question, we will be in a position to hear the word our text addresses to us. And then maybe we can also listen in a new way to that other lesson read earlier (John 14:15–31), through which the Church has traditionally proclaimed the Spirit's coming at Pentecost and the meaning of that event for us all.

We may begin with some obvious comments on the text in the more familiar setting given it by Matthew. You will agree, I think, that its opening sentences, when read in this setting, give ample cause for offense to anyone with even a modicum of critical judgment. When we are told that "everyone who asks receives, and he who seeks finds, and to him who knocks it will be opened," our response is apt to be as incredulous as when we hear those other words from Matthew's Gospel, "all who take the sword will perish by the sword" (26:52). Many an old soldier does not die by the sword, but simply fades away; and it is equally evident that wishing does not make it so. The gap, sometimes the unbridgeable gap, between what we ask for and what we receive—isn't it one of the facts of life of which we have each learned more than enough in the hard school of experience? And how many are the doors on which we have knocked again and again only to have them remain as firmly closed to us as ever? A full century after we fought the costliest war in our history to redeem the promise of our founding as a free nation, millions of our fellow citizens are still barred from entering fully on the rights thereby won for them—and that in spite of all the knocking on the doors of the intervening years.

True, it's just by presupposing such a situation to be possible among men that the text seeks to make its point. It takes for granted that men are evil and therefore are for the most part insensitive to the claims of their needy neighbors. Thus it argues from the lesser to the greater and tries to show that God responds to the petitions of his children with a goodness which is at best but adumbrated by the occasional kindness of sinful men. But surely the pleas of the Negro for the equal justice still denied him have not been addressed solely to those human councils that have been so slow to hear them, much less to grant them. Has he not also lifted up his voice again and again to the God of his fathers, the God of Abraham, Isaac, and Jacob, who once brought his people up out of bondage into the land of promise? And what of the unanswered prayers of those hundreds of thousands who were herded to their slaughter like sheep in the unimaginable hell of Auschwitz? Were their petitions for mercy and human kindness directed merely to the men who drove them to their death or passively witnessed it—or also to One who took upon himself all the incalculable burden of their suffering and pain?

Christians have always recognized, of course, that the question of unanswered prayer has its subtleties. Knowing that we are sinful men who do not know how to pray as we ought, they have been open to the witness classically expressed in the words of an unknown Confederate soldier:

> I asked God for strength, that I might achieve—
> I was made weak, that I might learn humbly to obey.
> I asked for health, that I might do greater things—
> I was given infirmity, that I might do better things.
> I asked for riches, that I might be happy—
> I was given poverty, that I might be wise.

ᒪ ᐃ ᘔ ᒪᒪ

I asked for power, that I might have the praise of
    men—
    I was given weakness, that I might feel the need
      of God.
I asked for all things, that I might enjoy life—
    I was given life, that I might enjoy all things.

I got nothing I asked for—but everything I had
    hoped for.
Almost despite myself, my unspoken prayers were
    answered.
I among all men, most richly blessed!

Yet, whatever the truth of these words—and where is the believer who would deny their truth—they do not remove the
stumbling block of Matthew's version of our text. To the contrary, they fully confirm it. "I got nothing I asked for," the
soldier admits. And that's just the point: so long as the content
of the promise is designated by the purely general and indefinite
term "good things," it is simply not true that "everyone who
asks receives," nor can we credit the claim, "Ask, and it will be
given you." So far as the good things of this life are concerned,
the gap between what we ask for and what we get can never be
fully closed. The plain truth of the matter is that some men ask
for a fish only to be given a serpent, and for too many the burden
of an unasked for and undeserved destiny seems all but to exclude
the possibility of honest faith in God.

    Thus we are reminded once again of the great tempta-
tion of all religion to pretend certainty about more things than
it should and to make promises that it does not have the right to
make. As Matthew presents them (perhaps unintentionally),
the words "Ask, and it will be given you" are an overextension
of Christian confidence. It is scarcely surprising then that they
are for many of us more of an obstacle to faith than a convincing
summons to it.

    But what of our text itself in the quite different
setting given these words by Luke. Is it, too, open to this
criticism?

Well, hardly. By changing Matthew's "good things" to the words "the Holy Spirit," Luke both avoids the difficulties that Matthew's version of the text raises and at the same time gives testimony to the unshakable confidence of Christian faith.

I mentioned a moment ago religion's perennial tendency to overextend the confidence proper to it by sometimes making claims that experience fails to justify. But this tendency is simply one particular expression of a deeper dilemma by which the whole of the religious life is threatened. If we are to think and speak of the Divine at all, it can only be by means of some kind of analogy with the nondivine realities of our experience. As the Transcendent or the "wholly other" in the strict sense of the word, God cannot become much more for us than an ineffable presence unless we in some way bring him within the limits of our ordinary thought and language. Either we must stand before him in virtual silence or else somehow seek to apprehend him in the same terms in which we must apprehend whatever it is given us to know.

Yet the great problem is that, in resolving this dilemma by choosing the second possibility, we only too easily forget the peculiar character of our religious thought and language. Concepts and words that can really be used only symbolically are continually misunderstood as having a straightforward literal meaning, with the result that God's radical otherness from us and our world is more or less seriously obscured. This difficulty is further compounded, then, by our universal proclivity to understand ourselves—or, rather, to misunderstand ourselves—in terms of what we are able to know and control, of what we objectively are and have and do. Instead of recognizing that the true meaning of our lives can only become real to us again and again anew through the honesty and integrity of our own personal decisions, we lose ourselves in the world of our experience and try to secure a meaningful existence by the good things with which it presents us. Health, wealth, reputation, and success become for us the indispensable supports of the only life that's really worth living.

It is this situation, implicit in the very nature of the religious life, which prompts the claim that "Christian faith is the end of religion." This claim does not mean that Christians somehow manage to think and speak of God other than in the symbolic way of men generally. Nor does it imply that they always succeed in avoiding the fateful confusion of God's essential gift and demand with the various good things in which men mistakenly seek the meaning of their life. The point, rather, is that whenever Christians are true to the faith that unites them, they preserve an acute sense of the radical otherness of God and refuse to domesticate him within the limits of their own knowledge and appreciations.

No one has seen this more clearly than the great American iconoclast, H. L. Mencken. "It is only the savage," he once wrote, "whether of the African bush or the American gospel tent, who pretends to know the will and intent of God exactly and completely. 'For who hath known the mind of the Lord?' asked Paul of the Romans. 'How unsearchable are His judgments, and His ways past finding out!' 'It is the glory of God,' said Solomon, 'to conceal a thing.' 'Clouds and darkness,' said David, 'are around Him.' 'No man,' said the Preacher, 'can find out the work of God. . . .' The difference between religions is a difference in their relative content of agnosticism. The most satisfying and ecstatic faith is almost purely agnostic. It trusts absolutely without professing to know it all."

Christians realize that what's chiefly wrong with literalism in religious belief is not just that it is hard pressed by an ever-advancing science, but that it robs God of his majesty as God. And more important, they know that God's primary gift and demand to men is never simply the good things in their world that they themselves can possess and dispose of, but his own personal presence and power—his own wholly free and all-embracing love in which the goods of life and life itself have their beginning and end.

The genius of Christian faith, in short, is that it lets God really be God. It breaks through the innocent and not so innocent idolatries of our natural religion and witnesses to us that the final meaning of our life is never to be found in that life itself or in any mere extension of it. Rather, faith claims that this meaning is solely the gift of God's love—in fact, *is* that love—and so is radically and qualitatively different from us and our world.

But one of the implications of this claim—indeed, I should say its chief implication—is that the fact of this gift, the fact of its having always been given to every one of us, is absolutely certain. Just because the final meaning of our life is not this good thing or that, but God himself, it is the one thing of which we may each be completely confident. For what makes God God, what radically distinguishes him from literally everything else, is that he is under all conditions bound to be and bound to be himself. Whatever other things may be or fail to be, God can never fail to be; and it is from the depths of his unfathomable love that these other things all proceed, even as it is to this love that they all at last return. Thus the great and final fact that the church speaks of as "salvation" is not merely one more particular fact besides the many others and continuous with them. It is, instead, the universal fact of God's never-failing love, in which all the particular facts are embraced, and which is the ultimate measure of their significance.

Just this, I believe, is the point of our text. It can assure us "Ask, and it will be given you," because the gift it promises us is not simply "good things," but "the Holy Spirit"—which is to say, God himself, his pure unbounded love, as personally and powerfully present in our own lives. Here, in this one unique case, the gap that otherwise obtains between what we ask for and what we are given simply cannot obtain, and the rule admits of no exceptions that "everyone who asks receives, and he who seeks finds, and to him who knocks it will be opened."

This rule, in other words, is exactly like those other promises which are so familiar to us from the Gospel: "Everyone who exalts himself will be humbled, but he who humbles himself will be exalted" (Luke 18:14; cf. 14:11 and Matt. 23:12); or "Whoever seeks to gain his life will lose it, but whoever loses his life will preserve it" (Luke 17:33; cf., e.g., Matt. 10:39). These promises, too, are always open to misunderstanding, and if we fail to see them in their proper setting, it is easy enough to dismiss them. Nothing is more obvious in our day-to-day world, where we compete with one another for the good things of life, than that the ambitious man who exalts himself is usually the very one who gets ahead, while to give up seeking one's life is simply to be trampled in the rush.

But the whole point is that it is not of this world that these promises speak. To the contrary, they speak to us of the utterly different reality of God and of our relation to him, and here they can never fail to be fulfilled. Here, in this one unique relationship, to exalt oneself is by that very fact to be humbled, and to seek to gain one's life is already to have lost it. By the very act through which we try to secure our existence in what we ourselves are and have and do, we are not only deceived as to our true situation, but are delivered into the hands of death, of that nothingness by which both we and our world are continually threatened. Henceforth the transitoriness of our life is no longer something merely natural, as provisional as life itself, but rather becomes for us the final power determining our destiny, and we must bear the awful truth that "on us and all our race the slow, sure doom falls pitiless and dark."

But the other half of the promises is no less sure of fulfillment. Just when we are willing to lose ourselves by humbly surrendering all our self-contrived securities, we can honestly acknowledge our actual condition, and God, instead of death, becomes for us the ultimate and determining power. Because nothing can be more certain than his love for us, to turn away from ourselves and our own transitoriness is in that very moment to be exalted beyond death into his eternal presence and to receive our life as a gift at his hands. As one of the mystics has put it unforgettably, "To await God *is* to possess him."

And so also with the promise of our text. It would proclaim to us faith's one great certainty of God's love and bid each of us so to ask for that love that he may really receive it.

This asking cannot, of course, be primarily a matter of words or even of fully conscious thoughts. The real prayer is never something merely verbal or reflective, but is the more elemental petition we are ourselves in our actual lives. To ask our heavenly Father for the Holy Spirit is to be open in our very existing to the presence and power of his love as our only final security. It is to acknowledge with honesty and integrity our own limitations and to be ready for the ever-fresh encounters through which both we and the world of our experience are continually transformed and made new.

And equally important to recognize is that our asking is the condition not of the Spirit's being given to us, but of our receiving it. Here, above all, we must be mindful of the symbolic character of all our religious language and not be betrayed into a false literalism. The whole point of our text is to let God appear in his majesty as God and to confront us with our possibility of life before him. But we would miss this point completely if we supposed that God chooses to become present to us only because we open ourselves to his presence. The only cause of God's love for us is God himself, and his decision that we shall be his people is always prior to our decision that he shall be our God. Therefore, in asking for his Holy Spirit by opening our lives to his presence, we do not initiate our relationship with him, but merely ratify it. We simply make fully our own the relation he himself never fails to establish by embracing each and every one of us in his infinite love.

Were it otherwise, the promise of our text would once again be made uncertain, and there at least could be a gap between our asking and our receiving. But the teaching of the text is clear, and it excludes all such uncertainty: "Ask, and it will be given you. . . . For every one who asks receives."

Yet surely this coming of the Spirit, which is promised to everyone who asks for it, is something different from the event the Church celebrates on this Pentecost Sunday. If we have rightly understood our text, its promise is universal. It witnesses to the reality of God's world-embracing love, and so to the possibility of his becoming present as the Holy Spirit to anyone who is willing to exist honestly before him. In our New Testament lesson, on the other hand, the emphasis at least seems to lie elsewhere. There the descent of the Spirit is represented as a quite particular event of the historical past, and his reception into our lives is made to depend on our keeping a specific word and commandments that are also historically given. Thus Jesus says, in the words read from the Gospel according to

John ,"If you love me, you will keep my comandments. And I will pray the Father, and he will give you another Counselor, to be with you forever, even the Spirit of truth" (14:15–17). Isn't the event foretold here something wholly different from the coming of the Spirit universally promised in our text? And isn't this event the real event of Pentecost?

If I decline simply to answer yes to these questions, it is not because I regard them as wholly mistaken. There is a difference here, and no one could deny that the event the Church remembers at Pentecost *is* the event which is the only source of its life as the Christian Church. And yet everything turns on rightly understanding this difference and on permitting this event to speak its own authentic word to us. My conviction is that our text and our lesson properly belong together and that they both acquire a new and deeper meaning when we listen to them in terms of one another.

When we hear our lesson in terms of the universal promise of our text, we are saved from a false understanding of the particular event in history whose meaning our lesson proclaims. We are enabled to see that the significance of Jesus Christ is not that in him God's Holy Spirit descends upon men for the first time, but that through him, God's universal outpouring of his Spirit has been decisively promised to us and that this promise has met with the faith of a believing community. Even in our ordinary relationships with one another, we recognize that a gift is fully given, really becomes a gift, only when it is received. In this sense, then, faith affirms that it is the event of Jesus Christ as known and proclaimed in the Church that the gift of the Holy Spirit is fully given. For in this event, God's universal offer of his love is actually received through a human word of promise having the same universal scope as that offer itself. "Ask, and it will be given you. . . . For every one who asks receives." It is this word, this completely universal word, that Jesus Christ both speaks and is, and it is because this is so, as Whitehead once said, that "the history of the world divides at this point."

But as surely as the meaning of our lesson is deepened by our text, it also deepens the text. It makes still clearer just how we are to understand that asking which we have seen the text to present as the only condition for receiving the gift of the Spirit. "If you would receive the Spirit of truth," Jesus tells the disciples, "then you must love me"—and that means, you must keep my commandments—or, as he also says, "You must keep my word." But what commandments, what word? Well, obviously, that of which Jesus is made to speak elsewhere in the same context in John's Gospel: "This is my commandment, that you love one another as I have loved you" (15:12; cf. 13:34–35).

Our lesson teaches us, in short, that the real test of our asking for God's Spirit is whether we are open in love to the concrete gift and demand of our fellowmen. If we are really ready for the Spirit, willing to live solely by the security of God's love, then the proof of such willingness is our openness to our neighbors, our readiness to hear their pleas for justice and human kindness, and to act so that God's love for them is concretely shown forth. This does not mean, naturally, that it is because we thus keep Christ's commandment that the gift of the Spirit is offered to us. No, in our lesson as in our text, the assumption is clearly that the offer of this gift has no other cause than God's own prior love for us as it is concretely disclosed to us in Christ. But it is solely where there is the earnest asking for this gift, and thus also the love of the neighbor which knowingly or unknowingly keeps Christ's commandment, that the offer of the Spirit is actually received.

What is the word, then, that our text and our lesson together would say to us this Pentecost Sunday? It is, I believe, the same word beautifully proclaimed by the German writer Ricarda Huch in her contemporary witness to the meaning of the Christian faith: "He who has not acknowledged the togetherness of men also has not acknowledged God, from whom all men proceed and to whom they return. . . . He who loves men is faithful and a child of God, even if he himself does not know it, yes, with words denies it. But he who does not love men is unfaithful, even were he to spend his whole life in the contemplation of God and an observance of divine commandments."

The asking for the Spirit to which our text summons us is not some special religious exercise, whether contemplative flight or formal observance, but that radical openness to God's love in our actual existence, which proves itself unmistakably by our own love and concern for one another. Wherever we actually ask in this way, *there* occurs the real event of Pentecost, the real reception of God's gift of his Holy Spirit—and that whether we stand within the Church, through whose word the gift of the Spirit is concretely promised to us, or only within that far larger community whose boundaries we as men are never given to discern.

The Curse of Abstraction

By W. B. J. Martin
Dallas College

Just before he died, the Scottish poet Edwin Muir wrote me a note. Oh, nothing important, confirming an appointment or something, but the note had a postscript, and poets' postscripts are worth other men's letters. Out of the blue, apropos of nothing at all, he wrote, "We are sick and we do not know it, or, what is worse, we know it only in the wrong way." Lots of people keep telling us we are sick, but "they know it only in the wrong way." Because their diagnosis is superficial or downright false, they only make matters worse with their pills and plasters and poultices.

Now Muir himself was convinced that what is wrong with the modern world is abstraction. "We are abstract men dealing abstractly with abstract matters." That, of course, is only my flat-footed way of putting it. He puts it more poetically and therefore profoundly. "The word made flesh is here made word again," he wrote. What was living and breathing has become for us bloodless categories, propositions, statements. We no longer care or know how to traffic with concrete particular things, but only with ideas, news, opinions. We see, no longer the thing there before us, but what we think we ought to see according to some theory we have read, some ideology we have embraced. We see not people—Tom, Dick, or Harry—but some abstraction called "believer" or "atheist," "radical" or "rightist," "Democrat" or "Republican," "pagan" or "Christian." No wonder Muir blazed out:

The fleshless word, growing, will bring us
  down.
Pagan and Christian alike will fall,
The auguries say, the white, the black, the
  brown.
The merry, sad, theorist, lover, all
Invisibly will fall. Abstract calamity
Save for those who can build their cold
  empire on the abstract man.[1]

Do you see those cold empires built on economic man, political man—abstractions all of them, but being abstract how easy to push around and manipulate and exploit?

Someone was pointing out the other day that the twentieth century is the most psychological age there ever was, and the least personal. Psychology should enable us to know more deeply, understand more profoundly, to forgive, to love, to appreciate, to enjoy our fellowmen; but it has become an instrument to exploit them, to trade on their fears, to steal their pocketbooks, and, worst of all, to evade them.

But we have our cold private empires, too, for even our homes and our love affairs today are built on such abstractions as teenagers, problem children, partners—partners, my God! No wonder Erich Fromm can say, "Love-making is usually a set of techniques by which two people manipulate each other for mutual gratification." I know homes where role—function—has so ousted the person that nobody knows the female parent's name—for she is always referred to as Mom, even by her husband.

But this love of abstraction goes deep. It always makes me laugh when I hear this described as a materialistic age. Materialistic? Not on your life! Our trouble is that we are not materialistic enough. If we were really honest-to-God materialists, do you think we would spend so much time on making a living, so little on making a life? Money, sheer money, is the most abstract thing there is, a mere token. Ah, but you say, we know that. We don't value money for itself but for the things it can buy. Yet isn't it odd that for every hour we spend making money, we devote five minutes to the things money is supposed

---

[1] This and other extracts from Muir's poems are reprinted from *Collected Poems* by Edwin Muir, published by Oxford University Press.

to buy—happiness, freedom, friendship, a growingly sick or exciting life.

Life! Abundant life! Everybody knows the familiar words "I am come that they might have life." Of course there is no such text. What Jesus said was—"The thief cometh not, but for to steal, and to kill, and to destroy: I am come that they might have life, and that they might have it more abundantly." The thing is not simply a claim, but a counterclaim, made in full awareness that there are theories of life, ideas, institutions, persons who impoverish us. And of these, the most deadly is the abstract noun, usually spelled with a capital letter, used to bully us into submission, I suppose.

You remember how E. E. Cummings hated the capital letter? He always wrote his own name in lower case letters? People talk about his eccentric typography. Was it he who was eccentric, off center, or we who persist in heralding our approach with those monstrous capitals, that great big "I" with which we call attention to ourselves? Humanists often spell God with a small "g." But notice that big "M" for mind—as if there were some thing called Mind apart from man's thinking! It is one way of reintroducing transcendence, I suppose.

Everywhere you turn you find sex spelled with a capital "S"—as if there were some thing, some substance, called Sex. There is no such thing as sex; there are only people, human beings, trying to find significance, to achieve fulfilment, to relate to others meaningfully and creatively. We talk about people being "highly sexed"—as if this man had two ounces of it and another a pound—poor fellow or lucky devil. But surely he whom we call "highly sexed" is the fellow who is trying hard to achieve meaning, significance, relatedness on one level only—who is too lazy or impatient to seek it with the wholeness of being. And so he exchanges the reality for the part, a part which in turn becomes increasingly abstract.

But let us get back to Edwin Muir. When Muir said, "The word made flesh is here made word again," he was mocking at religion. "Here" means the Church, the very place where abstraction should be fought like the devil, where man's full humanity should be prized and cherished and struggled for. Yet what happens? The churches somehow manage to turn out their own brand of "abstract man"—religious man, theological man—every bit as abstract as economic man or political man.

Muir was brought up in Scotland under a particularly harsh and colorless form of Calvinism—all book and no symbolism, all pulpit and no altar. Recalling his youth, he says:

> The word made flesh is here made word again
> A word made word in flourish and arrogant
>   crook.
> . . . .
> And here the mystery is impaled and bent
> Into an ideological instrument.

What he says here is that a person has become a proposition—his living speech in history and event has become statement and catechism, "brain-washing" rather than confirmation with man. But, of course, all that was forty years ago in the Outer Hebrides. Nevertheless, it still goes on.

Last summer, being a bit of a masochist, I attended a conference of theologians in Holland. Mercifully they spoke in English, but sometimes it sounded Dutch—double Dutch. And then it struck me. Of course, they were talking about "the Word of God." There's a great, whopping abstraction for you—the word of God, as if it were a thing, distinct and separate for God speaking, declaring, and manifesting himself how and where he wills. It so happened that I had taken George Russell's biography with me—George Russell, "A.E.," "A good Irish poet sicklied o'er with William Butler Yeats." Speaking of the sacred bodies of India, the East, George Russell said, "I have read them all and learned from all—the Geta, the Upanishads, as well as the mystic philosophers, Plato, Plotinus, Sankara. And I have found good in all, and a similar identity of belief." Then comes the payoff. "I found that the scriptures of Judea are the least interesting, the least profitable of all, being more a collection of tales and legends than a collection of sacred truths that are profound."

Of course! Of course! That is precisely the glory of the Bible. It is not a collection of sacred truths "that are profound," not an anthology of great thoughts, golden sentences, hanging in the air with no visible means of support. The Bible is a story—a sordid story in many respects, but it is the story of people encountering God in the rough and tumble of history, experiencing his dealings as they struggled to achieve nationhood, to exercise vocation.

Pascal was more perceptive than Russell. Remember how at Pascal's death they found the scroll in the bag about his neck? And on it the date, the day and hour of his conversion. And the mystic words, "Fire Fire Fire," and then the enigmatic sentence, "God, not the God of the philosophers and scholars, but the God of Abraham, Israel and Jacob!" God, the living God, not found at the end of an argument, but encountered in the concrete situations of life where men were most deeply engaged, involved, committed! This is what struck Pascal all of a heap, I think, not what God said to Abraham, Israel, Jacob. Did that apply to him? Does it apply to me? Maybe some of it does; some does not. But that He spoke, under what conditions, how man makes himself available to God, puts himself where God can get at him—this is all important.

I read the Bible not to find out what God said to Moses or Micah or Matthew, but because it is testimony to the God who speaks. I read his word there that I may recognize it wherever I am. Dear old Walt Whitman used to say in his easy way:

> I find letters from God, dropped in the street
> And every one of them is signed with his
>   name——
> And I leave them there, for I know others will
> Punctually come every day for ever and ever.

Oh, I like the nonchalance of that "And I leave them there." Not like the rest of us hoarding them, collecting them up, tying them in pink ribbon.

My friend E. Muir accused the churches of betraying the image:

> How could our race betray
> The image and the Incarnate One unmake
> Who chose this form and fashion for our
>   sake.

The word, the thing God is wanting to say, was made flesh, dwelt among us. He might have issued a statement, but he did not. "A statement was issued from the celestial White House." But it was not. Instead he confronts us in a person, in a life and death resurrection.

A statement binds. Have you ever tried arguing with a deep-dyed Communist, hearing the party line all the time? I once complained to Hugh McDemarist, who manages to be a Scottish nationalist and a member of the Communist Party all at once: "Hugh, why don't you talk to me man-to-man. You're always hidden behind that blessed ideology of yours."

"Same to you, boy," he said. "You've got your party line too, and you're paid to propagate it."

Well, if I believed that, I'd give up the ministry tomorrow. But there is a great difference between having a party line and facing a person. No great man I've ever met impoverishes me, and the greater he is, the more he liberates me to be myself. This has been my experience with Christ. And because in him the Word was made flesh, I am able to do something about that unfortunate, sometimes tragic, division of word and flesh in myself. For in us, these two are always at odds. The word—*Logos*—the principle of rationalism and form always at war with the flesh—the turbulent disorganized life within me. But in Christ I meet the God-man, not a centaur, half beast and half human, but a real man because related to God.

"No man hath seen God at any time," says the Scripture. And it is equally true that no God has seen men at any time. Man is the most arid, the most unreal abstraction there is. The least of my situation is that I am man hyphen something—man hyphen my family, peers, my land, my civilization. Always I am yoked.

I achieve live manhood when I am drawn into that relationship with God revealed by Christ and not only revealed by him, but made possible by him.

The Lights and the Light

By Kyle Haselden
Managing Editor of The Christian Century

> *Again Jesus spoke to then   ng, "I am the light of
> the world; he who follows me will not walk in dark-
> ness, but will have the light of life."*
> —John 8:12

"Jesus Christ, the Light of the World," was selected
months ago as the general theme for the Third Assembly of the
World Council of Churches in New Delhi, India. It was drawn
from our text for today and was therefore solidly grounded in
New Testament scripture. During most of the past year this
theme was studied in many parishes of the member churches of
the World Council in various countries of the world in preparation for the Assembly. These words were therefore the beacon
which drew 577 delegates, 49 observers, 105 advisers, and numerous other participants to New Delhi in the closing days of No-
vember and the early days of December, 1961. From all over
the world, across theological, traditional, creedal, geographic,
ethnic, organizational, racial, and political lines Christians
gathered to discuss, to serve, and to honor Jesus Christ as the
Light of the World.

Yet from the very first day of the Assembly this theme
diminished and others took its central place. Wherever else the
Third Assembly may have succeeded—and the successes were
certainly many and momentous—it failed its theme. The light of

116

the Third Assembly, as one delegate put it, was never turned up; the general theme became in fact the theme most generally neglected. The one clear note unmistakable in that theme—the uniqueness of Jesus Christ—was never boldly and categorically struck by an official Assembly document.

As a direct consequence, the message of the Assembly was a pallid thing—bloodless, tearless, and fireless and not to be compared to the message of Evanston and that of Amsterdam. And the witness section, paralleling those on service and unity, developed a declaration which, although repeatedly revised, never produced an enthusiastic response from the delegates. The last draft was finally and fretfully adopted by the Assembly as though conceding shamefacedly that it was better than no statement at all.

There was unity at New Delhi; all things considered, it was unity in astounding degree. There were evidences of ecumenical service at New Delhi; what the World Council of Churches does in interchurch aid and service to refugees, in the areas of rapid social change, in the fields of racial and interfaith tensions, in the bridging of international voids speaks louder than the Council says. But so far as any new, bold, unequivocal proclamation of Jesus Christ as the Light of the World was concerned, there was little witness at New Delhi.

Why so? To ask this question is to invite with it a host of unmanageable answers. Yet all of these answers, on second examination, have a striking similarity. One answer, for example, points to the overriding concern of the Assembly to protect at all costs the Council's newly gained unity. This concern influenced much of what was said, most of what was thought, and everything that was done at New Delhi; and this influence was usually dulcifying and sometimes deadening. Amsterdam was a birth; there the World Council came into being in 1948. Amsterdam was marked by the pain and labor, the excitement and joy, which attend the coming of a new being into the world. Evanston, when the Council met there in 1954, was a confirmation and it experienced the adolescent uncertainty, the confusion, the awkwardness, and sometimes the brashness with which youth reaches toward maturity. But New Delhi was a multiple wedding—the blending of two ecumenical movements and the uniting of many churches. If the prevailing spirit of the New Delhi Assembly was one of cautious deference, extreme courtesy, studied harmony, and the evading of such controversial subjects as the uniqueness of Jesus Christ, such a mood is characteristic of weddings. Why spoil the fun by taking up issues which can be postponed until later?

A second answer spreads this same mood into a larger area. India itself posed a problem for the Assembly. It was not the words "Jesus Christ" which troubled the delegates in the Indian setting. The delegates would not have been there if they had not in one way or another already confessed their faith in Jesus Christ as God and Savior. Nor was it the word "Light" which made the Assembly vacillate and temporize, for this is an apellation traditionally applied to Jesus Christ. Nor was it the word "World." India would not let the delegates forget the world lying outside the Vigyan Bhavan. No, the problem center, the monkey wrench in the Assembly's machinery, was the tiny, tough article "the." Should they stress it or let it glide, write it big or set it small? Should they say "Jesus Christ, the *Light* of the World"—an easy out in a land of many lights? Or should they say "Jesus Christ, *the* Light of the World" and face the charges of bigotry and exclusiveness which even a docile and tolerant Hinduism knows how to hurl?

You can see how such questions, raised in the Orient, raised in a land in which Christianity is still a feeble minority, in the India which has produced four of the world's eleven living religions—you can see how in such a setting such questions pose for guests the problems of elementary good manners toward their hosts. Even to ask the questions is to appear presumptuous, arrogant, bigoted. When several of the delegates visited a Hindu temple, the Hindu priest greeted them, saying, "Welcome in the name of our Lord and Savior Jesus Christ." Does not such courtesy and such inclusiveness require a reciprocal graciousness and an equal inclusiveness? Are we not permitted at times to slight the truth and forfeit conviction for the sake of amiability?

In New Delhi there is a magnificent modern temple built by the wealthy Birla family and dedicated to Hinduism and its derivative religions, Buddhism and Sikhism. Although on my visit to his temple I did not see the inscription, I have heard that among the many there is one inscription which reads, "Dedicated to the only true religion: Hinduism, Buddhism, Sikhism, et cetera." How tolerant and how harmless that appears and how boorish and arrogant Christianity would seem if in the face of such inclusiveness it should declare that it does not want to be numbered in the company of other religions or to take the place of "et cetera."

I talked all of one afternoon and late into one evening with a professor of the University of Delhi. We were not long in coming to the subject of religion. He was bright, eager, sensitive, and somewhat pathetic in his plea that I accept certain aspects of Hinduism even as he was quite willing to enshrine Jesus Christ in his Hindu pantheon. Then and there and together he and I, so he thought, could solve the conflict between Hinduism and Christianity by fashioning a mutually acceptable syncretism which would embrace both religions. Hinduism was willing, but Christianity was not. "Where, then," asked the Hindu, "is the tolerance you Christians talk about?" I confess that I had no instant answer, for I, too, am a genteel Christian and I was under the charm of the Assembly's accent on amiability.

For the true answer is a hard one. It is the blunt, un-apologetic claim that Jesus Christ is *the* Light of the World. Jesus Christ is not one among many holy men; he is unique, radically different from all holy men. However great such holy men may be, as unquestionably many of them are and were, the dissimilarity between him and them is a difference not merely in degree but in kind. He is not only a star of greatest magnitude in a constellation of similar stars. Far more he is the light itself which the brightest star can only dimly reflect.

This accent upon the uniqueness of Jesus Christ and upon the exclusiveness of his claim is undoubtedly offensive to the followers of other religions. If from our side Jesus Christ is in truth the "only begotten son of the Father," from their side this conviction is lumped with similar claims of other zealots. If we believe Jesus Christ when he says, "*I* am the light of the world," they in turn call such an audacious claim the ranting of a megalomaniac. If we say, with the apostle Paul, "at the name of Jesus every knee should bow . . . and . . . every tongue should confess that Jesus Christ is Lord, to the glory of God the Father," they reply, "Thank you for your offer and for your frankness. We are willing to comply if you will let us bow also to other names and confess other Lords."

So among Christians the question rises "Would not a more modest claim, a more courteous approach, a more lenient and inclusive attitude make the missionary task easier? Is it not better to have Jesus Christ saluted along with Krishna, Vishnu, and Buddha than to have him repudiated altogether? If the non-Christian religions are willing—as some of them are—to meet us halfway, must we not meet them halfway?"

The answer to that question is that certainly in one sense the missionary task of the Church—the evangelizing, witnessing task—would be simplified and made more pleasant if we did not have to insist upon the uniqueness of Jesus Christ and the exclusiveness of his claim. If we were willing to give a little Christ and take a little dharma, enlarge the Trinity to make room for Shiva, put Buddha's bo tree beside the cross and add Karma to Easter, then Burma and Ceylon might not enact legislation repressing Christianity, and India would welcome rather than resent our missionaries. Such adjustments, such adaptations, such modifications, would at once make Christianity acceptable and—destroy it.

The brilliant Hindu intellectual and Vice-President of India, Radhakrishnan has said, "Christians are an ordinary people who make extraordinary claims." Exactly. He meant it partly in derision, but it describes perfectly what we are. We are ordinary people. To approach the non-Christian world believing anything else, posing as anything else, is to evaluate their charge that we are bigots. Our faith makes us superior to no people, and our failure to keep the terms of that faith makes us inferior to no people. Moreover, it is not *our* religion which we offer to the world; it is the religion of Jesus Christ. It is not a Western religion which we profess. When that religion, born in Asia, first went east to India, our ancestors, the ancestors of most of us here, were still druids and cannibals. Nor should the proclamation of the Christian faith in any way imply that our culture, our government, our social philosophy, are the only way of life and must be adopted by those who adopt the Christian faith.

We are ordinary people; we are earthen vessels. The treasure we carry is the Light of the World. "But we have this treasure in earthen vessels, that the excellency of the power may be of God, and not of us." We are ordinary people, earthen vessels, and each extension of our ordinary humanness, however religious it may be, is an earthen vessel; our ecclesiastical architecture, our church polity, our hymnology, our religious art, and our philosophical systems which are for us the plinths upon which the faith rests—these are all earthen vessels. They are all expendable.

We can glorify God in gothic, colonial, and freeform churches, but they are not essential to the glorification of God. We can praise Jesus Christ in "A Mighty Fortress" and "Love Divine, All Loves Excelling," but these hymns can be replaced. We require harmony in prelude, anthem, and postlude; but Indian music, innocent of harmony, need not be lacking in worship. We formalize the truth we have received in philosophical systems which have a Hellenic origin, but the Oriental has other systems in which he can catch the same revealed truth. We are ordinary people and all our mental, emotional, and material extensions are earthen and expendable.

It was this fact—the fact of our ordinariness, our earthenness, our expendableness—coupled with the enormity of Asia's need for Christ which emboldened Oriental delegates at New Delhi to call for a freeing of Christian theology from the harness of Greek thought and logic. At the very outset of the Assembly a Burmese Baptist in the opening sermon pleaded for the right of the Oriental world to put the Christian faith not only into linguistic, artistic, and architectural forms indigenous to the Orient, but also into Oriental vessels of intelligence, logic, and consciousness.

In itself this suggestion did not raise a ripple of protest among the delegates. But when the Burmese Baptist illustrated his challenge with references to yoga, to the concept of the disciplined will, and to a theology which encourages the co-existence of opposites—yin and yang—and when he made lauda-tory use of the word "synthesis," this did cause alarm. Many of the delegates remembered as they sat listening under the sham-iana that they were met in a land where the master religion—Hinduism—had made a fine art of the techniques of absorption. They feared the possibility that the glutted sponge of Hinduism—still pliable, still receptive, and still resilient—would either dis-gorge an indigestible Christianity, as it did Islam and Buddhism, or envelop and obliterate Christianity, as it did numerous sects over scores of centuries. They knew, moreover, that the dual threat of syncretism or annihilation faces Christianity not merely in India but all over the East. The rising tides of nationalism in Ceylon, Burma, Pakistan, Indonesia, as elsewhere, have aroused the domestic religions from their lethargy and made them ag-gressive competitors of Christianity. The establishment of Hindu-ism, Buddhism, and Islam as national or favored religions in these countries has caused an identification of Christianity with the West and the evils of the West. By identifying the native religions with patriotism, these countries have put intolerable strains upon faithful Christians. These pressures are not always resisted. Some Christians desert the faith altogether; some ac-commodate their religion to the popular religions; and some Christians, not knowing how to live in their world without becoming a part of it, build mental, moral, and emotional ghettos into which they retreat. The Burmese's insistence that the uniqueness of Jesus Christ would not be challenged was not in this case sufficient.

But some of the Oriental delegates—D. T. Niles of Ceylon and Masao Takenaka of Japan, for examples—recognized the fact that syncretism—the adjustment of Christianity to the Eastern cultures and their religions—can become a rejection of the Christian claim for the inimitableness of Jesus Christ. They have seen what our American brand of syncretism has done to the Gospel and the life of Jesus Christ, how here Christ is ab-sorbed and dissipated by culture. They repudiated any such modification of the Gospel and reaffirmed their faith in Jesus

Christ as *the* Light of the World. But they insisted that Asian Christians must now break the pots in which the faith was brought back to Asia and transplant it in Asian soil. They insisted that Christianity must be cleansed of Western taints and freed from Western shackles if it is to live and flourish in the Orient. In part, these men were demanding that we remember—we Christians of the West—that we are ordinary men, that we are earthen vessels. We have the light but we are not the light.

Christians are ordinary people who make extraordinary claims. Yes, we make extraordinary claims. We claim as the scriptures do that Jesus Christ is *the* Light of the World, incomparable, irreplaceable, essential. We claim that he is brother to every man and yet utterly different from any man. We claim that in him and in him alone the fullness of the eternal Word of God became flesh and dwelt among us. We claim that at his name every knee should bow and every tongue confess that he is Lord. We make extraordinary claims, not for ourselves—God forbid that we should make claims for ourselves—but for that one who wills to be the Savior of all men and who, whether all men know it or not, is their Lord. The Christian faith recognizes no peers, accepts no substitutes. So far as rivals, aids, and duplicates are concerned, it is imperial, arbitrary, and intolerant.

We make extraordinary claims, and we must go on making extraordinary claims. It is not an easy thing to do, to be refined, sensitive to the feelings of other people, aware of our own disgraceful failures, alert to the good God stores in every life—to be this and at the time to make extraordinary claims. It is not easy.

But amiability does not release us from the compulsions of the truth; good manners do not free us from the witnessing obligation which Jesus Christ lays upon each of his followers. There is a radical difference between light and darkness, however dim the light, however deep the darkness. We therefore welcome all lights and respect them wherever they shine—in the face of the Jain who sells us a pair of shoes and earnestly talks while he sells of reverence for life, in the Sikh who in a polytheistic land worships a monotheistic God, in the Hindu who lets his religion—whatever we may think of it—permeate his whole being. A light is a light, and it is blasphemy to call it darkness.

But there is also a radical difference between lights and *the* light, between God's sons and his Son, between holy men and Jesus Christ. The light is the Light, and it is blasphemy for Christians to confuse it with the many lights. The syncretism which is guiltless tragedy for the non-Christians who have not seen the Light is a sinful tragedy for Christians who have. "The true light that lightens every man has come into the world . . . and the world knows him not." How sad it is that the world knows him not. But how shameful and how tragic when he comes to his own and his own do not receive him.

4

THE PROPHETIC CALL

The Brothers

By B. Davie Napier
Stanford University

Genesis 4:1-2 *Now Adam knew his wife, and she conceived and bore him Cain. . . . again: his brother Abel.*

I

One was a shepherd, one would till the ground;
one occupied the high land, one the low;
one practiced circumcision, one abhorred it;
one was contemplative, the other bold.
the one was one, the other was the other.

One was dark and one was light
one was brown and one was white
one was west and one was east
one was layman one was priest
one was soldier one was sailor
one a blacksmith one a tailor
one was dreamer one a doer
one a caveman one a wooer.

One was one and one the other
each to each a bloody brother
one liked desert one liked rain——
one was Abel . . . one was Cain.

127

128   B. Davie Napier

II

There's Abel over there, the fair-haired Abel,
the tight and tidy Abel—able Abel:
the ordered life, a time for everything;
existence neatly harnessed, firmly reined.

4:3–5 There's Abel over there, the backward Abel.
He stinks, you know, he literally stinks:
sweats too much and bathes too little,
fouls his streets with dunk and spittle,
the great unwashed. And arrogant! He thinks
that he is God's and all the world is his.

There's Abel over there, the odd-ball Abel,
Abel who differs—that's all right. But God,
how much he cherishes the difference,
not only in himself but in his God!
This Abel has devised an odd-ball God.
Of course I cannot altogether blame him:
no proper God—the Only God, that is—
would enter into league with such a man.
And what a spectacle my brother makes,
the brazen non-conformist, hatching plots
I know to seize the fruits of all creation.

I hate his guts, I hate the guts of Abel.
I'm sick of Abel, sick to death of Abel.

Sick of Brother sick of Fellows
Blacks and Whites and Browns and Yellows
sick of Negro sick of Jew
pressing pressing for his due
sick of white men bastard white men
arrogant and always right men
sick of sick men sick of sickness
Protestant- and Catholic-ness
sick of every lying bromide
Happy Birthday Merry Yuletide
freedom truth and brotherhood
Reader's Digest motherhood

pledge allegiance to the flag
"under God"—now what's the gag?

Sick of vicious ostentation
sick of humor's constipation
sick of sickness human sickness
human greed and human thickness.

Get my Brother off my back
White and Yellow Brown and Black.
Perish Abel perish quick——
One of us is awful sick.

III

4:6 *Why are you angry, why are you downcast?*
4:7 *If you do well, will you not be accepted?*

If I do well? What do You mean by well?
I am the very symbol of respect.
You know me, J. B. Cain, the president
of Acme Company; presiding deacon
of my church. They say I *am* the church
that no one moves a chair or gives a dime
belonging to the church without my knowledge
and my consent.

        Or let me introduce
myself, Professor Cain. What can I say
but what is said: noted authority;
writer of books and brilliant articles
dynamic lecturer, admired of students,
the envy of his colleagues. A modest man,
I live for learning and its meager fruits.
The adulation I but tolerate.
My one profession is the field of knowledge:
I spurn, for this career, all lesser goods.

If I do well? What do You mean by well?

I am a student, Sir, one of the best.
Jonathan Cain the Third. I chose this school

(as did my father Jonathan the Second
as did his father Jonathan the First)
and was accepted here because I have
the proper gifts, the proper attributes.
Not only am I here, but I belong
(it is enough to say that I belong).
The contours of success are everywhere
apparent in my person and my station.
I am the son of parents who are right;
I am the product of the proper schools;
I am myself the rightest of the right.

If I do well? What do You mean by well?

Meet Luther Cain, the bright young minister.
The servant, Sir. I love Thy kingdom, Lord,
the House of Thy abode. I give myself
to Thee and to Thy church. And no mean gift
it is. I am an honor graduate
of Christian University where I
was Student Council President and triple
letter man. (They called me "Triple-threat"
not in the mundane football sense, but as
a triple threat in studies, sports, and love.)
I come to Thee and to Thy service, Lord,
equipped in mind and heart—and in physique.
Together we will lead Thy people, Lord.

Why do You say to me, "If you do well"?
I am a doctor, lawyer, parson, teacher.
I am business man, Rotarian.
I earn an honest wage, I pay my bills.
I give to feed the poor. I hate what must
be hated. I support the decent causes.
I am a Mason, thirty-third degree,
Knight of Columbus, Synagogue and Temple.
I am a Man, first-born of Adam, son
of God, King of the Universe. A Man!

If I do well—my God, what do You want?

IV

4:7 *If you do well, will you not be accepted?*

Acceptance is it now? You toss that out
as if it were a simple thing: do well
and be accepted. *Ganz einfach! Voila!*
It does not work that way. To be accepted
or not to be accepted is the question;
and if to be accepted, on what terms,
whose terms, by whom, with whom, and to what end?

I know you, Chief. I know Your ancient problem.
The Word about Your nature gets around.
I know Your universalistic leanings;
I know that You are gracious, merciful,
in anger, slow, in steadfast love abounding.
This is, at least reputedly, the Word.
This is Your widely rumored reputation.

I hope you will not mind a mild rebuff:
deity should be made of sterner stuff.

You offer me acceptance, *on Your terms.*
You will accept me—if I come with Abel.
And this is what You mean by doing well:
hold my revolting brother by the hand.

Let me propose the terms. If You want me
You cannot have my brother. Damn it, Sir,
You know how rudely Abel comes between
the two of us. He fouls our sweet communion
where two is company and three's a crowd.
It is for You, for Us, I cut him off!
Besides, my way is difficult enough,
my passage rough enough, my risky crossing
frought enough with hazards of my own.

The choice to be or not to be accepted
is mine to make, and I have made the choice.
Acceptance on your terms is unacceptable:
As far as I'm concerned, Abel is dead.

V

4:8 *Let us go out into the field.*
Come, Abel, how shall I
kill you? Let me count the ways
since violence is versatile, and knows
not only overt savage acts of murder
but subtler forms as well, aesthetic forms
which spare the sight of blood but just as surely
remove the victim. Fratricide can be
grotesque or beautiful. Community
of brothers, sons of God, can be destroyed
in crude brutality or, if one will,
if one but exercise intelligence,
in fashion cold and clean and rational.

4:9 *So Cain rose up against his brother Abel
and killed him.* Yahweh said to killer Cain,
Where is your brother Abel? Where is Abel!
I do not know. Am I my brother's keeper?

VI

4:10 *What have you done? The voice of Abel's blood
is crying to me from the ground.* The voice
of Abel's blood, a thousand, thousand voices
crying to me from the bloody ground!

O Cain, my son, my son, who took the life
of Abel, son of mine. The voice of Abel,
the voice of Abel's blood, is crying to me
from the bloody ground, the blood-soaked ground.
O Absalom, my son, my son, who took
the life of Amnon, son of mine; the voice
of Amnon, Absalom, is crying to me
from the ground. O bleeding son of mine,
the son your brother (son of mine) despised;
my son rejected, smitten and afflicted;
my son, my wounded son, my dying son,
subjected to the public ways of dying
and all the countless private hidden ways——
in battle, execution, inquisition;

in lethal oven or in lethal humor;
in lynching by the hand of brutal brother;
or brutal psychological exclusion
(a quiet but effective form of lynching);
and always wholesale murder by neglect.

My son, my son! The voice of Abel's blood
is crying to me from the ground. O Christ,
O Jesus Christ, my son, my dying son!

VII

4:11–12 *Now cursed from the ground are you . . . it shall*
no longer yield its strength . . . a fugitive
and wanderer upon the earth are you.

4:13 *My punishment is more than I can bear.*
You curse me from the ground, the earth, the land;
the lovely land, the land of habitation;
the land of tent and temple, house and home;
the land of sound and singing; land of meeting;
the land of school and market; land of loving;
the land of birth and death and living passion;
the land of seeing, speaking, hearing, touching.

You curse me from the ground, and earth becomes
a curse and all its fullness—father earth;
productive mother earth; familial earth,
sister of faith and hope; consoling brother
of anguish; patient aunt, indulgent, loving;
the uncle bluff and crude and roughly hearty;
the frail grandparent, shrunken and unknowing,
but holding on to life and holding on;
the winsome cousin, gaily violating
the old taboos, and scorning inhibitions;
and tender lover, spouse, the close companion.

VIII

You curse me from the ground—You curse existence!
The lovely land becomes the loveless land;
relationships which ought to give support

are sour, insubstantial, charged with doubt;
the earth, the bloody earth, is unresponsive;
and I—I am a bitter fugitive,
a restless wanderer upon the earth,
estranged from Abel *and from You!*

From You,
You stubborn God! I can't lay hold of You!
From Your face I am hidden. Where are You?

Take back Your bloody earth, Your alien earth,
Your loveless, lonely, God-forsaken land.
This life, this bleak existence—this is more
than anyone can bear. So Come, Sweet Death!

IX

4:15 *Then Yahweh put a mark on Cain,* a mark
on everyman, lest man forget that he
is not his own but God's, made in His Image.
A fugitive he *is,* God's fugitive;
a wanderer he is, God's wanderer;
until the day when Cain becomes a Keeper,
when restlessness will be resolved in Rest,
and lovelessness in Love, and all estrangement
will be at last redeemed in Death.

X

Whose Death?
Whose Son?
Whose Brother?
Come, Sweet Death!

The World a Stage and We the Players?

By Sheldon H. Blank
Hebrew Union College–Jewish Institute of Religion

With your permission, despite my predilection for the Bible, I shall not this morning undertake to squeeze a biblical text. Allow me to try something different. Instead of squeezing a text, permit me to press an analogy. I know that pressing an analogy is not considered cricket, but I propose to press one all the same—to see what happens.

Shakespeare made the analogy, and he put it in the mouth of Jaques in *As You Like It*. Duke Senior comments on the piteous state of Adam, Orlando's ancient serving man. He says,

> Thou seest we are not all alone unhappy:
> This wide and universal theatre
> Presents more woeful pageants than the scene
> Wherein we play in.

To him Jaques replies with his famous analogy, "All the world's a stage. And all the men and women merely players." There's the analogy. Jaques goes on with his well-known unflattering observations on the seven ages of man. But we shall abide with our analogy.

All the world a stage, and we merely players. A good analogy. It appeals to the mind as patently valid and to the imagination as fruitful. But press it. Press it and observe.

135

We, the players. . . . Then there is a play. The play has been written, roles have been assigned. We move according to the action; we speak according to the lines. The director directs, and we enact our parts. *Is* that what I am doing here . . . and you . . . ? We wonder. In this latter half of this twentieth century, that is not, I believe, the mode of our thinking.

Press it again. If the play has been written, the end is determined. So why all the fuss? If the end is to be a kingdom of God on earth, why need we dream our utopias? Why spend our energies to shape a better world? If the end is the contrary—an apocalyptic cataclysm—why all our concern over fallout and thermonuclear warfare? And why should we pray? Yet we do; we do all of these. We dream our utopias; we work for peace; we pray. "Establish thou also upon us the work of our hands," we say. "Yea, the work of our hands establish Thou it."

Squeeze the analogy a final time. A play must have an audience. If "all the men and women" are "merely players," who then are the audience? Who are the men and women who watch the cosmic play—for what is a play sans audience? You and I—where do we fit in? Are we strutting on the stage, or are we sitting in the gallery or dress circle?

The question is not without meaning in this mid-twentieth century. You and I—do we not again and again appear to ourselves as just this, as the audience at the play? Are we not players at all, but audience—spectators only, powerless to affect the unfolding drama? Is that not indeed, the sickness of our times—this sense we have of being left out? For our generation, the world is not cosy; it is no intimate theater; from the far-off gallery seats one can barely hear the lines.

But still the question, Where do we fit? Are we merely players on a world stage; are we merely audience; or is there, perhaps, an option beyond these alternatives? This, I suggest, is a question worthy of a little thought: players, audience, or what? May I take you with me briefly into my classroom and show you how a student's query helped me find a provisional answer to this question? (Thank God for the students who go on asking, who are not to be put off with easy answers.)

In the classroom I speak of, I deal with the Hebrew prophets, with the nature of men like Amos, Micah, Isaiah, Jeremiah, prophets who lived in the eighth, seventh, sixth pre-Christian centuries and addressed to their people words which that people preserved, words which now form the heart and living core of the Hebrew Bible. In that classroom I have repeated courses year after year for a number of years; and so it is perhaps strange that not until a few weeks ago had a student ever asked the question that made me take the second look that helped me stumble onto the thought I want to share with you.

To begin with, it is a matter of rhetoric. I had often noticed and called attention to the rhetorical feature of prophetic discourse to which in my classroom I give the name of "irony"—"prophetic irony." You may have noticed it yourselves. Irony is present when prophetic words have a double meaning, two meanings—one for the people, another for the prophet. The people find comfort in a phrase, the prophet catches overtones of menace and grief. You will sense the irony in the prophet's voice when I give some examples, but before I do so let me say that what I had been hearing in all such passages was bitterness and nothing more. To me their tone was simply sarcastic carping. What now I hear is something else—but of that later.

That the prophets in question were sharp critics of their society goes without saying. They saw about them evil doings and in God's name condemned the evil-doers. They denounced the rich for their rapacity, the nobles for their unconcern, all men for their sham piety. But not the least among the fatal faults that they denounced was the harboring of inherited delusions—delusions fed by an easy faith in an indulgent God.

It was largely these delusions which were the target of the prophets' barbed irony. These delusions were the field on which prophetic irony grew. One who frequently resorts to irony is the prophet Jeremiah. And one of the best-known examples of his irony is his denial that the presence of God's temple in Jerusalem is an insurance policy, a guarantee of that city's safety. "Do not rely on delusions," he said. This was precisely what his people were doing; they thought God needed and wanted the offerings they brought him there and their songs of praise; they thought they could buy security. "No," Jeremiah said. "Do not rely on delusions and say: The temple of God, the temple of God, the temple of God are these." And he continued in God's name: "Will you steal, murder, commit adultery, swear to falsehood, sacrifice to Baal, go after other gods whom you knew not and come and stand before me in this house . . . and say: We are safe?"

Long before his time, another prophet had attacked the same delusion in words to be remembered. "The people of Jerusalem," Micah had said, "countenance bribery in the courts, venality in the church, corruption in high councils, and yet In God they trust and say: Is God not here with us? No harm can possibly befall us."

I thought that I understood the grim and horrifying irony of passages such as these—of which there are many—in which people fondly recall past victories as precedents for newly anticipated triumphs only to shrink before fresh blasts of prophetic irony. That is the sense, is it not, of a passage in Isaiah where the prophet alludes to the popular hope for victories—for such victories as the Lord gave to Israel in more ancient times when he miraculously intervened "on Mount Perazim" and "in the valley of Gibeon." He alludes to this popular hope ironically, so that we may convey his sense with some such paraphrase as this:

> The Lord will rise up now as he did then on
>   Mount Perazim [*you hope*].
> He will fume again as he did in the valley of
>   Gibeon [*you wishfully think*],
> To do his deed; *well so he will*
>   but strange will be his deed;
> And to finish his work; *you are right again,*
>   but alien will be his work.

With acid irony Isaiah seemed to be saying that the Lord indeed would fight but, dismayingly, on the wrong side; he would, I almost said, carry the ball across the wrong goal. He seemed to me to be saying this and no more.

Until I looked into the meaning of irony. A student asked, and I looked again more closely at the meaning of irony. I found that what I had in mind has a technical meaning and that its proper name is "tragic irony." Consider its nature and you will know what bearing it has on our question: players, audience, or what? Properly, tragic irony appears when the audience knows what the players do not. The masters of tragic irony were the classic Greek tragedians, notable among them Sophocles. The audience, viewing, for example, a performance of *King Oedipus*, is in on the secret. Oedipus does not know the meaning of the cryptic oracle, but the audience knows—naturally so, because the tragic tale of Oedipus and his dire fate belongs to their ancient common tradition. They know what man is doomed, who must be driven from the land. They know the name of the unknown murderer whom Oedipus blandly curses; they know it grimly well. They know the course of events, know in advance the outcome of the action. Given such circumstances, what the actor does or what he says has meaning for the viewers that it cannot have for him. In a comedy or a farce this produces laughter; in a tragedy terror. Viewing a classic tragedy, probably the audience sat silent and helpless, suffering along with the plundered protagonist.

Where then does tragic irony reside? Who experiences the irony? The players or the audience? The audience endures the tragic irony—the audience beyond the footlights, equipped with all the knowledge and the sympathy but not the means to avert the tragic climax. Tragic irony is the pain built into the dramatic situation, the pain the audience endures.

When I had come that far in my new understanding of the term, I asked myself again what, if anything, this tragic irony might have to do with the irony of prophetic discourse. Clearly, I said, prophetic irony is tragic irony. But what are the terms and the relations? Here is what I found.

This is what I am adopting as a working hypothesis: that the prophet is audience, his people the players. The prophet is audience; this I had not understood. He is audience; he it is who looks on in mounting horror as the action unfolds. As in a performance of a classic tragedy he, the audience, knows what his people (they are the protagonists) do not know. He, the prophet, knows because he has been told, because he is a prophet, in his terms, God has told him. And so, as he watches the players and hears what they say, their words have a different meaning for him—different because he knows the end of the play. Therein lies the tragic irony, as I am beginning to see.

But at this point I pause and observe a proper caution. How far may I press *this* analogy, I ask. Admit the parallel, there still is a significant difference between the audience viewing the classic Greek tragedy and the prophet witnessing the unfolding tragic fate of his people. The prophet cares, and this not simply because he must count himself among the doomed and would save his own life (an earthquake is not selective), but because he is actively concerned on his people's behalf. The prophet cares; he is more than a suffering spectator, helpless in horrified silence, suffering the chills of catharsis. The prophets cared; it is a fact not to be overlooked that the prophets loved their people. They pitied and prayed for them; they lamented and wept as they contemplated the looming terror.

"God's angry men" is not a term that I would use for the Hebrew prophets. The prophets cared. Though with power and vigor and grim realism they condemned the insensitive rapacious oppressors, they were not simply angry. Though with unvarnished words those prophets denounced all social evils and threatened dire disasters, they could yet pray. They could yet weep, and that same Jeremiah that relentlessly predicted the ruin of Jerusalem with the exile of Judah, imagining his people already in exile, could lament,

> Lo, the sound of the cry of the daughter of
>   my people
> From a distant land. . . .
> Is there no balm in Gilead?
> Is no physician there?
> Why has there not been found
> Healing for the daughter of my people?
> Would my head were water
> And my eyes a spring of tears!
> Day and night I would weep
> For the slain of the daughter of my people.

Those were such words as Jeremiah often spoke and not he alone among the prophets. All were sensitively involved with the grief of their people. The prophets cared.

They cared and they shouted. The salvation of their people was their concern and their program, and speech was their medium. They did not bottle up their concern; they shouted. And so, although the analogy is just, and the prophets may be compared to the audience at the tragedy, they are yet to be distinguished from that silent, helpless audience, and though prophetic irony is like tragic irony, it is not merely that. The parallel is not perfect.

I have taken you with me, I hope, to the classroom. But we are not now in a classroom. This is a chapel, and I have a lesson to bring. What, let me ask now, has all this to do with you and with me?

With this question we return to our starting point. Is all the world then a stage with all the men and women merely players? Are we "merely players"? Where do we belong? Are we players, or what?

Ask first of all who, then, "we" are. You and I, who compose this college community (as your guest speaker, allow me today to include myself), who are we? Consider our self-image. We are not simply "all the men and women"; we are the students and teachers, men and women of a great university with a proud liberal tradition, men and women with a living sense of history and a far perspective, dedicated to progress in science and the arts, cherishing a sense of responsibility—one commensurate with our deepened understanding, men and women religiously oriented, for, though God may not be speaking to us in a voice we recognize as his, in place of that word of God we own a tested religious tradition.

If that is who we are, then what are we? Are we "merely players" foredoomed by the action to move inexorably onward to a tragic close? Are we simply spectators sitting in open-mouthed horror, weakly watching, powerless to affect the outcome? Or may we compare ourselves—respectfully admitting the distance that divides us from them—in a certain sense with the

Hebrew prophets, involved as they were, and as surely we are, with the human scene, more than players, more than audience? We are audience and something more—the more that moved the Hebrew prophets.

As they were of the people, so, too, are we, and our self-interest lends us concern. If an earthquake is not selective, neither is an atomic warhead. Projecting our anxieties, we count ourselves among the doomed. We who are trained to see beyond battles cannot exclude the vision of an armageddon—a last day for man on earth. He is now the protagonist. There is a final curtain lowered in our lifetime, closing off our lifetime, leaving this earth to the insects. But, like the prophets again, because of a sympathy beyond self-interest, a sense of mission, a love of man, we also harbor concern. We want to affect the outcome; we want to help write the play.

Like the prophets, we want not only to preserve our world (that it should not revert to chaos) but to better it as well. Our eyes still fixed on the ancient utopian ideal, we are not content and will not be content until men are free of fear, and free of want, until they may "sit every man under his vine and under his fig-tree" with none "to make them afraid." What is is good, we say; we treasure life and say that it is good. But we will neither be coerced nor yet seduced to the thought that this good is good enough.

If we think that men are not in essence depraved but that being made, as we say, "in the image of God," they share a limitless potential for good; if we think that what men imagine in their minds, the faith they hold, the creed they confess, is indeed important but that it is infinitely less significant than the doings of their hands which that faith inspires; if we think—if we hope, at least—that a rational purpose moves the world but that what *we* bring toward the fulfillment of that purpose is a vital contribution, so that it ultimately matters what we do; if we pray: "Establish thou also upon us the work of our hands; yea the work of our hands establish thou it"; if these are our thoughts and our prayers, we cannot count ourselves as "merely players" in a finished script. Neither can we sit idly content as spectators gaping; rather must we speak as prophets spoke, voicing our passionate concern.

If concern is anyone's business, whose business is it more clearly than ours? If there is a place where we may legitimately look for thoughtful men and women who care, surely this chapel is that place.

Judge Not

By *Theodore A. Gill*
World Council of Churches, Geneva, Switzerland

Christians are always putting grubby hands on profundity. We are not the only ones, or even necessarily the worst ones, to do this, but over and over again we take ultimates and vulgarize them. Some hear a commandment about not taking the name of the Lord our God in vain and turn it into an obscene attack on *Catcher in the Rye*. Some take a concern for freedom and turn it into vigilante denial of any radical difference. Some read a text with all the interior significance, the psychological resonance of "Judge not," and exteriorize, trivialize it into a bidding of etiquette.

Actually, of course, the injunction "Judge not" is not a matter of personal manners. Instead it is a strong lead toward a solution of the problem of the Christian life, a lead toward an answer for the question of what the Christian life truly is. The problem is, What makes my life "Christian"?

The question is, Is there a certain kind of life, is there a certain kind of action which is recognizably Christian and which we all ought to emulate and copy and imitate if we are going to be Christians? Is there a recognizable entity—the Christian life? Ought we all, insofar as we are Christian, to be acting the same, thinking the same, doing the same, reacting the same? Is there one pattern of righteousness to which all of our lives will conform, which will fit all of our lives if we are really Christian, or insofar as we are living really Christian lives? Is there one silhouette

144

which all of us will occupy if we are Christians? Is there one common profile which all of us will fill out to the last little jog and niche? This is the question of the Christian life, then.

Now it seems to me that the sense of Jesus' injunction "Judge not" answers this question about the Christian life with a resounding negative. No! There is no pattern for the Christian life. The Holy Spirit is not a homogenizing agent. Every Christian personality is certainly not like every other Christian personality, nor like any other Christian personality. There is no spiritual colander through which all of us are pressed when we become Christians, thus equalizing our temperaments and attainments. We are different before we are Christians, and we are different after we are Christians. The new man may be a new creation, but he is neither mass-produced nor machine-tooled. He is custom-built, with no more violence done to his temperament than to his physique. We are as different temperamentally and physically and dispositionally within the Church as without. There is no mean man, no average man. We do not have congregations full of mean men and mean women. We have congregations full of characters. You do not sit before me as several hundred identical prints of one archetypical, capital-M Man. You sit before me in all the wonderful, bewildering variety of several hundred very shaky small-m men. We are all different. It ought to be no surprise, therefore, that the Christian life is realized and evidenced differently in each one of us.

Once upon a time we got the idea that to live the Christian life is to obtain a certain level of objective, observable goodness, and then to stick there. That is what it is to be a Christian. Here is goodness way up here—you work, you struggle, you fight your way through until you get way up there, and then you hang on there, and that is living the Christian life.

But what we have to admit now is that that never was a Christian attitude. As a matter of fact, Christianity is not even involved in bankrupting that idea. Leave Christianity clean out of the judgment. That particular idea still will not go. The point is, it is not even fair—much less Christian. Because, you see, what we know about ourselves now, thanks to analytic procedures and the publicity about them, is that all the things—the private things—that we thought were only our own anxieties are everybody's anxieties. Now we know that all the little worries and nagging shames and guilts and uncertainties that each of us thought were his alone are everybody's. Only no two combinations are the same. So we account for the universality of individual men and for individuality in the universe of men.

Now that we know that we are all in the same boat in this thing, that we are all mixed up by the same things, only each in his own mixture, now we know and can face the consequent fact that it never was fair to say there was one level of objective, observable goodness to which you got if you were good. Because now we know that some people have never had much trouble getting to that level and maintaining that level. Their dispositions and their temperaments and their glands co-operated. And others could try their whole lives through and they never get even near that level, never get off the floor, because their dispositions and their temperaments and their glands resisted. And they did not choose their temperaments any more than they did their physiques or their glands. These are part of the given, part of the creation; these are set when we all start. And some start ahead and some do not. Can you then say that there is any equity in this idea that we all get to the same place and hang on there or else we are not Christians? Leave Christianity out of this. This is no theological question. It is just ordinary, humanistic equity that is involved here. You cannot say that those first swimming ones were Christian, and the second, stuck-to-the-floor ones are not Christians. As I say, that is not even fair. You're crediting what almost could not be helped and you are blaming what was largely an accident.

Or we could go at it another way. We would all admit, surely, that there is no special virtue in rising from some excess or other, completely worn out with it, fed up with it, and vowing never to do that again. It would be no significant accomplishment to come stumbling out of some fleshpot or other, utterly exhausted by it, muttering that you'll never go there again. The resolution from satiety does not count. The morality of revulsion is not significant. The ethics of exhaustion is not moral. But just so, now, neither does untempted goodness count. A lack of temptation does not count morally or ethically whether it comes at the beginning as disinterest or at the end as exhaustion. It is wonderful socially, physically, if you do not steal or commit suicide. But it is not even significant from the point of view of the Christian life if you don't ever want to steal or commit suicide. In terms of the Christian life, you are not getting anywhere especially or proving anything particularly by compliance with laws that do not bother you or by eschewing sins that do not interest you. Doing what comes naturally and not doing what does not come naturally has very little relevance to the Christian life.

John Donne's preaching was a little gustier than most of our fancy Dan preaching today—maybe a little more robust than our tender Christian sensitivities can take any more. But in one of the great days of preaching, on this point old John Donne said, "Chastity is not chastity in an old man, but the disability to be unchaste. Therefore thou dost not give what thou pretendest to give for thou hast no chastity to give him." But we Christians have been awfully good at pretending that this kind of a gift was a really significant one. And just think of all the other areas where we do the same thing—take credit for not doing things that never occurred to us to do, that we don't even really like the idea of doing. But we think to chalk down our sour abstention on the plus side with the Lord.

> We compound for sins that we're inclined to
> By damning those we have no mind to

The original beatniks in my home town used to talk about going out to sex and homosex. Many tidy Christians were appalled by the phrase—and even more by the facts. It is perfectly true that there was nothing very elegant about either the expression or the intent. But let us be very careful how we take credit for our refinement and disgust. If you are one of those willowy ones of languid body temperature, whose boiling point is way high even under the most heated conditions, just be careful how much credit you take for your noble dating reticence which may be due at least as much to ductile deficiencies as to Sunday school scruples. And if, on the other hand, you are one of those insistently robust buckos who never had an ambivalent thought in his square head and simply cannot understand this strange new unilateral love that seems to be sweeping the place, do not, do not take special spiritual credit for despising the boys who apparently like their vice versa.

Doing what comes naturally and not doing what does not come naturally have very little relevance to the Christian life. If they did—if goodness, if the Christian life is somehow objective, something you can see and describe, if it is a certain minimum achievement, if the degree of one's Christian living is the degree of one's compliance to some laws or compliance to some pattern—then I say to you that the state of your Christian life will depend in large part upon the state of your frontal lobes or the kind of grandmother you had or what happened to you on a subway when you were five (or did not happen to you on a subway when you were five) and how your enzymes happen to be flowing at any particular moment. That is where you get, now, if you have any truck with the old idea that goodness is an observable, objective level. This is where you are driven, inevitably, if you are going to say that. If the Christian life is one common structure of action, then virtue is glandular. But it is not. The Christian must not agree that it is. That means that we cannot admit that the Christian life is a level at which we arrive and where we try to stay. Once you do that, you have landed yourself in a determinism that leaves no room for the Gospel, that makes all the rest of our talk about what we have been proud to call the Christian religion beside the point.

The Christian life is not a single level at which we all arrive and where we all try to stay. To say that it is assigns overwhelming importance to the individual temptations, drives, and compulsions which constitute me, me and you, you. No, the Christian life is not a state of being into which you can or cannot settle, depending upon what your physical, temperamental equipment is. That old image of the Christian life as conformity to a pattern is passé. That is impossible. It never was any good, never has really been adequate, but we have gotten along with it one way or another and some lives have been given a certain strained radiance by the effort to comply—and a lot more lives have been smashed by it, bulldozed and steamrollered by the terrible uniform demand. It is no good, I tell you, and I can't tell you dispassionately. I have known and loved too many of the victims of that "Christian" life: wonderful, juicy human beings who were persuaded by a misguiding Church that they had to veil their vividness, bank their fires, dehydrate their interests, denature their enthusiasms, if they wanted to be Christian.

No, the old idea will not do. I am not altogether sure which new one will do. But I would suggest that maybe we could get ahead by saying that the Christian life is to be thought of more in terms of the direction of our aspirations and our actions. It is what we do, the way we move in our doing, our temptations, our drives, our compulsions being whatever they are. That will be different for each of us. If there is any hopefulness in this, of course, you must say immediately that it is not going to be how far you get in the designated direction that counts. Because as soon as you start saying it is, you have all the old problems back in again. How far you are going to get in that direction will depend on all those old accidental factors again. So using distance as a scale of achievement imputes too much importance to the accidental factors. Not distance, not how far we get in that direction, but how we keep headed in that direction no matter what happens—that is what counts. We posit, I hope, at least this much content and meaning to what we call freedom.

Lest anyone think that such suggestion is novel doctrine, let me insist that, on the contrary, what I have been trying to elaborate here is a base upon which all ministers have long proceeded regularly in their pastoral counseling. At least I hope that no Christian minister has ever confronted any man who came to him in trouble with the pattern of what perfect righteousness ought to be in every case and then smashed him on the pattern. Christians do not do that. All I am really pleading for is that the Christian ministry bring into the pulpit some of the assumptions upon which it operates in the office.

Think of any congregation now. Think about the good woman in that church (the conspicuously good member of the congregation is ordinarily a woman). A pillar, she is—there early to get the flowers in the vases, and there last to "close the

church," as we say. You know the one. She *is* a good woman, too.
I am not trying to be snide, now. She is always there, in the same
pew, in the same place, every Sunday. She is a leader—a real
leader: several times president of the Ladies Aid, and what is
even more important, long-time treasurer of the Missionary Society. She is every woman's idea of the Christian they would all
like to be—or so they always say. She is the one. "Oh, if we could
only be like Mrs. So-and-So. She can pray. Right out loud she can
pray. You can call on her any time, and she can stand up and
pray. It doesn't bother her a bit. Don't you call on me to pray.
I'll come to your meeting, but don't you call on me. But Mrs.
So-and-So can always pray. I mean she's really. . . ." Now I am
not laughing at her. We all know who she is, and God knows we
would not get far without her. All I am suggesting, I am sure, is
what all of you have thought from time to time. Have not you
sometimes wondered what any ultimate judgment might be like
on such a life? Whether in the long, long run, considering everything that has been in favor of this woman, considering how little
resistance there has been inside or outside . . . cannot you imagine
some ultimate judgment really marking this lady very low for not
having been far more, done far more than she ever did with what
was given her? With the favors and graces and opportunities,
with the clear way before her, inside and out? It is artificial; it is
abstract; who knows that much about anybody? But the possibility, I am sure, is a real one: the possibility of disappointment
rather than satisfaction over the good woman—disappointment
that she was not more creative in her goodness, that she was so
prematurely satisfied, and divine disappointment with the
Church that has let her be so satisfied with this easy occupation
of the traditional silhouette, the conventional pattern of what
righteousness is.

On the other hand, everybody will know who in the
congregation is the reprobate (a man, of course, if he is a reprobate). The one who comes to the First Protestant Church just
a little late (when the processional hymn is being sung) because
he can slip in that way while everybody is standing up and not so
many will notice he is there. The one who sits back behind a
pillar; the one who knows perfectly well when he enters and when

he sits down that there are those who know him and what he is, who will be saying to themselves in their most reverend diapasons, "What does he think he's doing? Doesn't he think we know what he does at night?" If it is bad, it is at night, of course. Again, has it not ever occurred to you that it is at least remotely possible that in some grand assize this man, too, far from being marked low, as his fellow Christians judge him, may be marked rather high. To think that he would even dare come this time to this church! Extraordinarily enough, might not this be an achievement that the good lady with squatter's rights down on seventh row center will never come up to in a whole lifetime of being good and fixing the flowers and praying right out loud? Considering all there is against him, inside and out, what he knows about himself, what he knows others know about himself . . . is it not a spiraling achievement that he should have made the effort at all? This is the kind of consideration that makes a statement like "Judge not," far from being a cliche about human manners, but a plain statement about very plain fact. Of course, "Judge not." On what can you judge? How do you know how to judge? It is not just the mote in your own eye. It is just the opaqueness of that other person to you, to anybody but God. Of course, "Judge not." You cannot judge. You do not have it to judge on. So lay off.

Again John Donne. "A poor man may have heaven for a penny who has no greater store. But God looks that he to whom He has given thousands should lay out thousands upon the purchase of heaven. The market changes as the plenty of money changes: heaven costs a rich man more than a poor because he has more to give." The image is commercial, but Donne is not talking about money.

Well, let me now try to say the whole thing once more another way. It seems to me that for all too long a time it has been thought that the Christian life was a life lived within a legalistic box. The life that could fit within the boundaries of that box was a Christian life. The laws were the walls of the box; thou shalt, thou shalt not (two sides), thou shalt, thou shalt not (two sides), thou shalt (bottom), thou shalt not (sealed top). There is the Christian life. You get inside the laws, you fit inside that box, and then you are living a Christian life. Whatever of you hangs out, whatever appetite or interest or urgency, whatever hangs out, whatever doesn't fit has to be lopped off . . . chopped off. So the truncated life becomes the Christian life. The cut-off, the hacked at, the bruised and bleeding, life—this becomes the Christian life. This has been the Christian life for too long a time for too many people in too many places. Christianity then becomes one long exercise in repression and compression and pinching and parching. This is the Christian life. If we do not conform to the pattern, we are not Christians. At least we are not living the Christian life.

But what we see now is that some by accident of birth, or nature, or by freak of circumstance some just do fit naturally and some just do not. Some curl up in the middle of the box and stretch as they will; they cannot even touch the walls. I do not call them lucky. And there are others who could try from now till Doomsday and they could never cram themselves into that box. In neither case were all the determining factors anything that they had everything to do with, or about. Many of the determining factors are the givens, are the creation, are where they started. They do not start with the same things, at the same place, or with equal propulsions or drags. How, then, can you use the box for any kind of judgment? Of course, "Judge not." You do not have it to judge on or to judge with. This is not a wheedling plea. That is not a coaxing of Christians: please do not be hard on each other. This is a plain statement of extra-plain fact. You do not have the goods to make this judgment, so cut it out. Some just do fit naturally in the box. Other just do not. If you are going to say that the former are Christians or are living the Christian life, and that the latter are not, then I am warning you, you are predicating a double predestination more vicious than anything that Calvin or Gottschalk or Augustine or St. Paul (it pleases a Presbyterian to be able to share the blame) ever dreamed of. The classic proponents of a theological predestination boast, at most, of an election to an eternal destiny, but this traditional view of what the Christian life is finally comes down to a physical determinism which the theologians of election would not have been caught dead espousing.

So I say we have to abolish the whole picture of the box. The Christian life is not the life that is made to fit the legalistic box, that is forced to fit into the pattern. The Christian life is life lived in a certain direction—in, through, around, above, whatever temperament, physical, psychological obstacles any of us may have. But always in that direction—the direction which is assigned to us by what we know of God, by what we know in Jesus Christ of the character and nature of the realest real, by what we know in Jesus Christ of God, and the love of God. The Christian life is life lived in appropriate reaction to God's action for us. This assigns us a direction. A theological shorthand would suggest we call this a loving direction. It is the direction of love. This is the way we ought to aim our lives. The life aimed in this direction is the Christian life. Again, for each, the level of objective, legalistic achievement is going to be different, according to his physical, temperamental equipment. But for each the Christian life will be real and significant and full, depending upon how consistently he manages to keep heading in that direction. Not how far he gets but how consistently he manages to keep heading in that direction, not how far he gets but how consistently he gets back—that is what counts if anything counts.

Maybe this parable at the end will clarify what could be still a confusion. Some few of you have characters and careers that make a straight, level, green-turf track on which the Christian personality runs the race of the Christian life like a hundred-yard dash. Fast and direct and easy—and more power to you. Others of you have characters and careers like a cross-country course with hills and dales—sometimes in the clear, sometimes in the woods. Here the Christian personality will run the less comfortable, slower race. The rest of us have characters and careers like an obstacle course with traps and hurdles, hedges and mud holes that make the running rough and tough and dangerous. The race the Christian personality will have to run on such a course will be at best a twisting, turning, stumbling, falling affair, involving nose dives and pratfalls aplenty. It will be hard, but it will be exciting all the way. The courses will be different, then, but the end is the same. The important thing is not how far or how fast we go—that will depend on the kind of track each of us draws, on the particular equipment each of us is issued, and we do not have everything to say about either. The important thing is not how far or how fast we will go, but that we keep going. For the Christian life will be described not in degree of attainment, not with the kind of common judgment we use too often, the Christian life will be described in terms of the direction we are headed and of how well we keep going in that direction no matter how often we trip and fall.

But Not Yet Free

By Carlyle Marney
Myers Park Baptist Church, Charlotte, North Carolina

When Jesus spoke of "truth" and "freedom" to "those Jews which had believed on him," they claimed they were already free since "we be Abraham's seed and were never in bondage to any man." They lied or were blinded. For Jews had belonged to Egypt, Assyria, Persia, Greece, and Rome. In their blind adherence to the notion of their inherited freedom they lost the freedom they did not know they lacked and that Messiah had to give.

Freedom is not an inheritance; it is an achievement. "Freedom," said Paul Scherer in Austin, "is not so much an inalienable right as it is an interminable quest." And now, strange to our ears is Jeremiah's old cry, "The harvest is past, the summer is ended, and we are not saved." How like those ancient Jews we are.

Even our slogans about how free we are become marks of our slavery. By and large, the world over, we live in the Hungarians' "twenty-fifth hour," and our refuge is not always a true temple of God. Here in modern America, for millions, the refuge is a new kind of padded cell.

We live in a world of locks and burglar alarms, pistols, and railroad detectives. We go for cedar-lined closets to protect us from insects and wind insurance to buy off the storms. Our lives are dependent on bank vaults, credit ratings, and retirement plans; we live with bulging medicine cabinets, hospitalization

155

contracts, slats under bedsprings, belts and suspenders, too. Cancer, heart attacks, and wrecks; these are our fears. Credit, debts, compensation—these are our concerns, and the drive is for security. Give us status, property, security; guarantee it with federal funds. Make sure life turns out right.

In order to bulwark this security, we carry around with us a swarm of comfortable notions: chosen people, the voice of the people is the voice of God, private Zions, the superiority of a certain racial minority, the invincibility of American arms, the virtue of American character, the value of the material, the worthwhileness of all business, belief in the temporal, belief in the future. And the goal? Happiness. Make sure life turns out right. And if it does not? If the going gets rough? There is always a portable padded cell from which millions can dodge the sharp edges of reality.

Every pastor knows, and all laymen are aware—we are witnesses, even participants, in the unhappy spectacle—the center of material prosperity and technical development becomes the rule of Whirligig the King. Frenzied by the pace, we breathe faster, run harder, buy more, drink more, crack up oftener, and bury quicker. And in place of our vaunted freedom appear the hard edges of a new padded cell: barbiturates to sleep on, caffein to wake up on, tranquilizers to calm shot nerves, Pepto-bismol to slow down juices and ulcers, hydrochloric acid to speed them up; aspirin for minor insulation, Demorol for a blackout, beer to break the ice, vodka to melt it.

And God? No longer standard equipment, he becomes for millions the Great Accessory to whom there is little occasion to turn save as one wants to get or forget, and in the mass of pornography piled just inside the drugstore door one can take his choice of Norman Vincent Peale or Mickey Spillane, who do very well the same job of guaranteeing for the moment that we will not have to face reality, and if TV in the corner isn't enough, we can carry a portable to clutter up vacations. But this is a surface view. There are bars on our cell.

Out of five hundred years of our life and work in a world of machinery, men have learned to expect "things to go right." We now expect the same tireless, efficient output from our liver and lights that once we could get only occasionally from gadgets. Surgeons must perform successfully like automatons; friends should respond instantly like telephone bells; marriage is a mechanical harnessing of personal powers; salesmen exist for output; recreation is measured by quarts and sizes; profits are guaranteed, while sons and daughters are mechanical toys. God is essentially a mechanic, but what is worse, mechanics are gods. The great high priest is the service man who, like God, is on duty twenty-four hours a day; and if he is in TV, automobile, or air-conditioning repair, only God can help him unless he is available and good. In this wing of the padded cell the distinctively human is swallowed up in the distinctively mechanical. And we are not free.

Again, how easily all men fall into the error of thinking of the world as an enlarged copy of their own village. Fettered to our own provinces, we are almost never aware of the power of the ideas that hold us in geographical, cultural, political, ideological, economic, religious, and personal thralldom. Nor do we recognize easily our involvement with ideas not native to our soil, and it does not seem too strange to find German isolationism in Texas, Confucian ideas in current philosophies of education, Hitler's Nordic man in the Cumberland Mountains, the Ku Klux Klan in churches, Yankee supremacy among Americanized Chinese, economic determinism among Communist-hating bank directors, Americanized Fascism on some school boards and among some college trustees, cannibalism in business, Anglo-Saxon notions of superiority in mission fields, Shinto ancestor worship in distinguished families, Catholic authoritarianism in the mores of free churches, and laboratory pragmatics in religious education. So confined we are; we think we thought it all up and do not know our debts and heritage, good or bad, to the Orient and to Europe. The wheelbarrow was a new and untried idea to Queequeg in *Moby Dick*; so he picked up barrow, baggage, and all and carried it on his back to the inn. How many notions we carry not our own. How many bars on our cell.

Even the institutions men rightly cherish can bar them from Gospel freedom. "We shape our dwellings, and afterwards our dwellings shape us," confesses Churchill. Men like the safe protection of ordered surroundings and do not wish truly to be free. Rather we want things and people labeled, so they will not slip around and jar us too much. This is true especially with respect to society, politics, and religion. We lean on our institutions to keep from leaning on ourselves, and so cluttered up can life become in the emotional matters of race, politics, and faith that a man may live eighty years and never learn what is truly valuable or who he is. In all his institutional involvements both the valuable and the personal have been swallowed up, and we are not free.

And worst of all, everywhere men, by and large, are centered in themselves—a denial of freedom.

Kierkegaard tells of a peasant who came clean-shaven to Copenhagen and had such a load of wood to sell that he could buy himself a pair of shoes and long stockings with enough left over for a glorious drunk. As he was trying in his drunken state to find his way home, the peasant lay down in the road and fell asleep. Much later he was awakened by a teamster shouting down at him, "Move, or I'll drive over your legs!" The sleepy peasant looked at his legs and not remembering his new shoes and stockings cried, "Drive on! They are not my legs." This is the sin of the world. We do not know our own legs—that every man's agony is our own agony. Business is business! Might is right! If you can, do. We will not risk truly belonging to each other. Each sets out after his own and will never run the risk of having been a fool.

And when it's over? "Yes, yes," says Unamuno. "I see it all . . . an enormous social activity, a mighty civilization, a profuseness of art, of industry, or morality, and afterwards, when we have filled the world with industrial marvels, with great factories, with roads, museums, and libraries, we shall fall exhausted at the foot of it all, and it will subsist—for whom? Was man made for [this] or was [this] made for man?"

We confess that we are born-again-to-be-free. We confess that we will not submit to the chains that bind our world and us. We confess that the freedom-in-obedience that God intends us to have is within our reach. We claim that by faith we shall be free, for the master of life has promised us mastery.

We know that every search for truth and freedom has bred its own heroes, for in the very words two of the primary nerve centers of human desire are exposed. Their raw edges push us to seek, and the prospect of truth and freedom always winsomely beckons or imperiously drives. Every search, I say, has bred heroes we do not forget: the biological quest, the economic, the technological quests, the nuclear, the biochemical, the astronomical quests, the mathematical, the philosophical journeyings, the psychological, the medical, the theological— every search has its values and its heroes. But we know, with Berdyaev, that there are truths and the truth—truth which is beneficial, truth which is ruinous; and there is saving truth which is personal, and therefore a Person. It is of this saving Person, Christ, no other, that our text speaks. How impossible is this verse for library doors and university hallways. This saving, freeing truth implies a Person of peculiar mastery over life. Its resultant freedom is not the philosopher's freedom. Luther saw this, too, and translates with the simplest German word available: *frei*—to be untied. Jesus used the word again with reference to a colt, the foal of an ass, when he said, "Loose him, and bring him to me."

It is a mistake to treat these words "freedom" and "truth" as if Jesus were a philosopher. True, he used two words of tremendous import in all philosophical discussion, but once again Luther's translation is right: Here "truth" is the simple fact, the deed, the thing in its ramifications—and "freedom" is "to be turned loose."

This is the uniform spirit of the New Testament. The truth is the person, Christ. Thou art the Christ, the Son of the Living God; Christ is Lord; Lord Christ; that one who would come; God was in Christ reconciling the world unto himself— and hath committed unto us. . . . These are the words of the New Testament understanding of truth, saving truth. Ye shall know the truth—the fact, the thing that is, the deed, the *wahrheit*, the very is-ness of "God in Christ reconciling by cross," and this will "turn us loose" to have power over life.

"Loose us." Yes. But from what? The Gospel truth in the Person Christ is to release us from idols, from our slaveries, from ourselves and our sin, our shallow localisms and ideas, our smug false superiorities and assumptions of special blessedness along with our crass dependence on Mammon (the things Jesus warned most against) and our absurd care. Loose from these? Indeed we are not yet free.

Ye shall know God in Christ involved in our suffering, and this will turn you loose. To do what? To be rid of sin forever? Not so, not hardly, and not yet. For once more Luther precedes us on the path to freedom, for after his high burst of temper against Anabaptists and all extremists and the rabble of the peasants, he was to lament *"Semper justus; semper peccator."* He found it strange to be justified of his sins, but not yet free of his sinning.

Loosed? To do what? In the holy boldness of my knowledge of myself as sinner, I am released by this matchless Person to have power over life and ideas, over institutions and provinces. I need no longer be a mechanical little man performing my marvels in obedience to the pressures of mere tools and institutions. I am, in this Gospel, elevated to where I can see the difference between the tools and the work itself; the end becomes more important than the tool or the means, and I become a man living in a kingdom of ends, no longer the slave of tools I pick up and lay down.

But more. This freedom gives me victory over suffering and death. If truth is the Person, everything that minimizes, warps, or cuts off persons is untruth. This is not to say that evil does not really exist, but it is to say it cannot endure forever, nor can it hold confined forever the eternal persons now involved with evil. This is why Christians can be manly about the facts of this present world. We know we have to face bluntly and biologically both suffering and death. We do not expect to be spared the agonies of suffering and death. Grief-drawn Luther turns away from the burden of preparing his little girl for her death.

> *Magdalenchen, my little girl [he had said], you would like to stay with your father here and you would be glad to go to your Father in heaven?*

Yes, dear father, as God wills.
Du liebes Lenichen, you will rise and shine like
the stars and the sun. How strange it is to know that
she is at peace . . . and yet to be so sorrowful.

In the face of this death, we hear no stirring "Yaah," as with his own death—only Luther calling on Christ, as must we. But you know what? In the face of suffering and death, we find ourselves borne into the realm of a higher and grander reality and sometimes we even feel redemption flowing out of our own agonies-in-Christ to the need around us, and we claim the ultimate victory in the strength of this Person who personalizes us. But this freedom does not come to all. There is a condition without which the promise of the text is absurd: Ye shall know God in Christ involved in our suffering and this will turn you loose only "if ye continue in my word." And that condition one does not find carved over doors. For "continuing in his word" has always been a controversial matter. To continue in his word puts everything we know and love under terrible judgment. To continue in his word calls us to shoulder a fearful responsibility. It forces us to sense the larger room that lies beyond our cardboard cells and makes us want to enter in, but we fear the cost of too close an inspection of our valuables and our concerns. To continue in his word would deny us the worship of our machines, the fever for the immediately available, the grasp of the known value, and our love for ourselves. To escape the cardboard cell, to deny slavery by admitting we are slaves, to come in to the truth of personality and the freedom of release comes high; it means the death of desire for security and the birth of passion for life at its highest—but most clearly it means the acceptance of a burden we have never really claimed—the burden of the sins and needs and hurts of the whole world. This is at once our deepest need and highest challenge.

Salvation—which means everything God himself can do for the whole world—has always been such an "individual" blessing for us. We have received it by grace; we are quite willing for God to give it to all men just like us. But we have never really "continued in his word" by making Christ's burden our own. We have never truly felt ourselves sent to shoulder the burdens, with all Christians, of the whole world. This we have evaded by calling it a "social gospel" when there is no such thing. There is only a half-gospel which preaches the needs of the world to the exclusion of the needs of single men; and there is another abortive gospel, just as malformed, which preaches individual redemption without the aspect of our being involved for and with and in Christ at the business of seeing the whole of things redeemed. Christ died for the sins of the "inhabited world of men," according to the Scriptures, but there are principalities and powers which undergird the kingdom of evil against which we not only have never led a major assault, but which we have connived to keep in power.

Here in America an amazing fortuity of circumstances has brought us to a power we hold nowhere else in the world. The frontier life, the appeal to people of a particular economic level with energy to "rise in the world," the preaching of a gospel for common man with its clear emphasis on individual repentance, confession of sin, salvation by grace, a church of the people, and for twenty years now, an unprecedentedly energetic and effective work of evangelism in the churches and the mighty powers of a vast co-operating constituency have brought us to where we approach majority strength in our whole section. Even among the inmates of your state penitentiary those of Protestant persuasion probably hold the lead. Consequently, responsibility for every continuing social ill, for every agony of poverty, vice, crime, provincialism, prejudice, and corporate evil lies closer to our door than we dare admit, and so lies the power to change things.

The corporate life of mankind is our business; the agony of little children is our business. The viciousness of laws old and new, the carelessness of institutions, the evils of many business ventures, the ungodliness of advantage-taking advertisement, the devastating moral and personal corruption of alcohol and drug interests both legal and illegal, the awful cancer of race and class advantage-taking are all the business of Christ who died to lift us all. And if we follow? If we see this—if we can cross the thorn-studded barrier into the larger room of universal concern for all, we are not "social-gospelers," we are a New Creation.

What a dream. The laity of the Christian world, a new creation, committed to the acceptance of a cosmic burden, to the expansion of our horizons, to the confession of our slaveries and our needs, to the judgment of our culture, and to the exploration of a road no company of men have ever had a better chance to see and follow. This is Gospel freedom.

The best recipe for hell I know is to stand by on the assurance of one's own salvation, as if one could belong to Christ and have no part in Christ's work. To miss this is to remain bound in the hell of staying forever as we are.

I grew up less than an hour from William Wallace and could have known him, but I did not. He was martyr stuff years before his death, but I did not know him until he was dead. It seems strange to me now that I came to know of Wallace through a Roman Catholic priest, then pastor of Corpus Christi Church in Oklahoma City. We, the priest and I, were members of a preaching mission at Oklahoma A. and M. College. By the priest's invitation, I heard his address at a convocation of hundreds of Catholic students. At the close of his winsome and simple presentation of what to me was an incredible, pre-Copernican world view, the carillon in the tower over us broke out in a mighty burst of bell-ringing. Presently I caught the theme of the music and outside the hall I had to roar with laughter. Of all the hymns in all the books, some ignorant but well-meaning carillonneur was rolling out Luther's Battle Hymn of the Reformation to close the Catholic convocation. It was too good to keep, and that night I told it before the twenty of us, and Father Walde had the grace to think it a good joke and threw back his handsome, shaggy head and laughed too.

But next morning it was the priest who paused at my door to share with me the section of the *New York Times* which printed the letter of two Roman missionaries which gave the details of the death of their fellow prisoner, Dr. William Wallace. The priests said that they had a common desire to bear witness to the details of a death they had shared and felt Baptists and the free world would want to know how Wallace was strangled in his cell.

Where else but at some point of shared suffering could Walde and Wallace and I come together? And where else but at that point of common agony, the Cross, can we find impetus and strength for what we have to do. In the birth of our common desire to bear witness to a death we share lies our truth and freedom.

The Good I Will, I Do Not

By Paul Tillich
The University of Chicago

> *For I do not do the good I want, but the evil I do not want is what I do. Now if I do what I do not want, it is no longer I that do it, but sin which dwells within me.*
>
> —Romans 7:19–20

"I do not do the good I want, but the evil I do not want is what I do." Is this the way we are? Do we feel correctly described by Paul's words? Is the split between willing the good and achieving it as radical as the words of our text indicate? Or do we resist this indictment, replying that we often do the good we want and keep away from the evil we do not want? Is not Paul grossly exaggerating the evil in man in order to give a dark background to the bright foreground of grace? These are questions every critic of Christianity asks. But are they not also questions *we* ask, we who call ourselves Christians—or at least people who desire to be what the Christian message wants us to be? Actually, none of us believes that he *always* does the evil he would like *not* to do. We know that *sometimes* we do the good we *like* to do, an act of love to a person with whom we are not in sympathy, or an act of self-discipline for the sake of our work, or an act of courageous nonconformity in a situation in which it endangers us. Our moral balance sheet is not so bad as it would be without these acts. And did you ever see a preacher of what is called the "total depravity" of man who did not show in his own behavior a reliance on a positive moral balance sheet? And perhaps even Paul did. At least he tells us so when he boasts about his sufferings and his activities in a letter to the Corinthians. Certainly, he calls his boasting foolishness; but wouldn't we also call our hidden boasting to ourselves foolish? We would, and nevertheless we would not stop boasting. We even call people who believe that they have nothing to boast about sick, disintegrated, without self-esteem, objects of pity or counseling. But perhaps they are not really like that. Perhaps even they are proud—proud about the depth of despair in which they see themselves. Without a vestige of self-esteem no one can live, even if his self-esteem is based on the despair of himself.

But why do we not then dismiss the words of Paul, why are we impressed by his statement that I do *not* the good I *want* to do? Because we feel that it is not a matter of balance sheets between good and bad to which those words point, but it is a matter of our whole being, of our situation as men, of our standing in face of the eternal, the source, aim and judge of our being. It is our human predicament that a power has taken hold *over* us which is not from us but *in* us, hated by us and at the same time one which we gladly accept. We are fascinated by it; we play with it; we obey it. But we know that it will destroy us if we are not grasped by another power which resists it and is able to keep it down. We are fascinated by that which can destroy us, and in some moments we hiddenly desire to be destroyed by it. This is the way Paul saw himself; this is how many of us see ourselves. It is a picture not unlike the one we are often asked to have of ourselves. People who call themselves Christian parents, teachers, preachers tell us that we should be good, obeying the will of God, and for them the will of God is not much different from the will of the socially correct people whose conventions they ask us to accept. If we only willed it, they say, we could achieve such goodness and would be rewarded in time and eternity—but first of all, in time.

One can thank God that such preaching has become more and more suspect, for it does not strike at the real human situation. The eyes of many serious persons in our time are opened to the awareness of their predicament as men. Every sentence in Paul's message is directed against the so-called men of good will. They are the ones whom he sees under a power which drives them to act against their "good will." And *they*, that is, *we*. For who amongst us is not full of good will? But perhaps if he knows himself, he may become suspicious that this good will is not so good after all but is driven by forces of which he was not aware.

Shall I describe people who embody good will and the working opposite hidden under their goodness? Psychologists and others have done this so fully that it needs no repetition. Despite what critics say against our time, one of the great things to come out of it is the difficulty of anyone being able to hide permanently the motives of his actions from himself and others. Whatever we think about the methods in which this insight has been reached, the insight itself is infinitely precious.

It as become difficult for a man who works incessantly with dedication and success in his business or profession to be assured about the goodness of his doing. He cannot hide to himself that his commitment to his work may also be a way of escaping genuine human commitments and, above all, a way of escaping himself.

And it has become difficult for a mother who loves her children passionately to be assured that she has only *love* for them. She cannot hide from herself that her anxiety about their well-being may be an expression of her will to dominate them or a reflex of a deeply covered hostility which desires to get rid of them.

We cannot applaud every act of moral self-restraint, knowing that its cause may be cowardice preventing a breaking through inherited, but already questioned, rules of behavior. And we cannot applaud every act of daring nonconformism, knowing that its cause may be the inability of a man, especially a young man, to resist the persuasive irresponsibility of his group.

In all these and countless other cases, we experience a power which dwells in us and directs our will against itself.

The name of this power is "sin." Nothing is more precarious today than to mention this word amongst Christians as well as non-Christians, for there is a tremendous resistance against it in everyone. It is a word which has fallen into disrepute. To some of us it sounds almost ridiculous, providing a source for jokes more than for serious consideration. To others who take it seriously, it sounds like an attack on their human dignity. And again to others who have suffered under it, it is like the threatening finger of a disciplinarian, forbidding what they would like to do and demanding what they hate to do. Therefore, even Christian teachers, including myself, shy away from the use of the word "sin." We know how many distorted images it produces. We try to avoid it or to substitute something else for it. But it has a strange quality. It always comes back. You cannot get rid of it. It is as insistent as it is ugly. So it is more honest—and I say this to myself—to face it and ask what it really is.

It is certainly not what men of good will would have us believe it to be—a failure to act in the right way, a failure to do the good one should and could have done. If sin were this, a less aggressive and a less ugly term, such as human weakness, could be applied. But this is just what sin is *not*. And those amongst us who have seen demonic powers within and around themselves find such a description of sin ludicrous. And we turn to Paul, and perhaps to Ivan Karamazov in Dostoevski's *Brothers Karamazov*, or to the talk between the devil and the hero in Thomas Mann's *Dr. Faustus*. There we learn what sin is. And perhaps we learn it through Picasso's picture of that small Basque town "Guernica," which was destroyed in an unimaginably horrible way by the demonic powers of Fascism and Nazism. Perhaps we learn what sin is through the disrupting sounds of music which do not give us restful emotions but the feeling of being torn and split. Perhaps we learn the meaning of sin from the images of evil and guilt which fill our theaters or of the revealing of unconscious motives which fill our novels. There we can learn what sin is. It is a noteworthy situation that today, in order to know the meaning of sin, we have to look outside the churches and their average preaching to the artist and writers and ask *them*. But perhaps there is still another place to learn what sin is, namely, our own heart.

Paul seldom speaks of sins, but he often speaks of Sin—Sin in the singular with a capital "S"—Sin as a power controlling world and mind, persons and nations.

Have you ever thought of Sin in this image? It is the biblical image. But how many Christians and non-Christians have seen it? Most of us remember we were taught at home, in school, and in church that there are many things one would like to do, but one should not do. And if one does them, one commits a sin. We also remember that we were told of things we should do, although we did not like doing them. And if we did not do them, we committed a sin. We got lists of prohibitions and catalogs of commands, and if we did not follow them, we committed a sin. Naturally, we committed one or more sins every day, although we tried to reduce them with much seriousness and good will. This was, and perhaps still is, our image of Sin—a poor, petty, distorted image, and the reason for the disrepute into which the word "sin" has fallen.

The first step to an understanding of the Christian message which is called "good news" is that we dispel this image of Sin which is equated with a catalog of sins. Those who are bound to this image of Sin are hardest to reach by the message of acceptance of the unacceptable, the good news of Christianity. Their half-sinfulness and half-righteousness makes them unsusceptible to a message which states the presence of total sinfulness and total righteousness in the same man at the same moment. But these people always have something to show on which they base their self-confidence. They never find the courage to make a total judgment against themselves, and therefore, they never find the courage to believe in a total acceptance of themselves.

Those however who have experienced in their hearts that Sin is more than the trespassing of a list of rules know that all sins are manifestation of Sin, of the power of estrangement and inner conflict. Sin dwells in us; it controls us and makes us do what we don't want to do. It produces a split in us and makes us lose the identity with ourselves. Paul has written of this split twice in a short space: "If I do what I do not want, it is no longer I that do it, but Sin which dwells within me." Those who have experienced this split know how unexpected and terrifying it can be. Some thoughts entered our mind; some words poured out of our mouth; something was done by us, suddenly, without warning. And if we looked at what happened, we said, "It could not have been *I* who acted like this. I cannot find myself in it. Something came upon me I hardly noticed. But there it was and here I am. It is *I* who did it. But this *I* is a strange one. It is not my real, my innermost, self. It is as if I was possessed by a power which I hardly knew could reach me. But now I know that it not only can reach me, but that it dwells in me."

Do we really know it? Or have we, after a moment of shock, repressed such knowledge? Do we still rely on our life as we live it, comparatively well ordered, avoiding situations of moral danger, determined by the rules of family, school, and society? For those who are satisfied with such a life, the words of Paul are written in vain. They refuse to face their human predicament. But something may happen to them. God himself may throw them into more Sin in order to make them aware of what they really are. This is a bold way of speaking, but it is the way people with profoundest religious experience have spoken. They felt the hand of God awakening them by being thrown into more sin. And awakened, they saw themselves in a mirror from which they always had turned away. Now they could no longer hide from themselves. And in the depth of their self-rejection, they asked the question to which the Christian message is the answer, the quest for a power of acceptance which overcomes the despair of self-rejection. So, more sin *can* be the divine way of making us aware of what we are.

We then ask with Paul, What is it within us which gives a dwelling place to this power? He answers that it is in our members that Sin hides. He also calls this place flesh, and sometimes he speaks of our body of death. But there are also resisting forces in us, our inmost self, our mind, our spirit. Using these words, Paul wrestles with the deep mystery of human nature, just as we do today. And it is not any easier to understand him than to understand our present scholarly language about man.

But one thing is certain. Paul, and with him the whole Bible, never has made our body responsible for our estrangement from God, from our world, and from our own self. Body, flesh, members, that is not the *one* sinful part of us, with the inmost self, mind, and spirit comprising the *other*, sinless part. But our whole being, every cell of our body, and every movement of our mind is both flesh and spirit subjected to the power of Sin and resisting its power. The fact that we accuse ourselves proves that we still have an awareness of what we truly are and therefore ought to be. And the fact that we excuse ourselves shows that we cannot acknowledge our estrangement from our true nature. The fact that we are ashamed shows that we still know what we ought to be.

There is no part in man that is bad in itself as there is no part in man that is good in itself. Any Christian teaching which has forgotten this has fallen short of the height of Christian insight. And here all Christian churches become guilty. They must all share the blame for destroying human beings by casting them into despair about guilt where there is no guilt. In pulpits, Sunday schools, and families Christians have called sinful the natural strivings of the living, growing, and self-propagating body. They concentrate in an inordinate, purely pagan way on the sexual differentiation of all life and its possible distortions. Certainly, these distortions are as real as the distortions of our spiritual life, as, for instance, pride and indifference. But it is itself a distortion if the power of Sin is seen in the sexual power of life as such. In this way, such preaching completely misses the image of Sin as Paul has depicted it. What is worse, it produces in countless persons a distorted guilt feeling which drives from doubt to anxiety, and from anxiety to despair, and from despair to escape into mental disease and the desire to destroy oneself. Still other consequences of this preaching about sin become visible. Paul points to the perversion of the sexual desires as an extreme expression of Sin's control of mankind. Did we as Christians ever ask ourselves whether through the defamation of the natural as Sin, or at least as a reason for shame, we did not perhaps potently contribute to this situation? All this is a result of that petty picture of sin which contradicts reality as it contradicts the biblical understanding of man's predicament.

It is dangerous to preach about Sin because it may induce us to brood over our sinfulness. Perhaps one should not preach about it at all. I myself hesitated for many years. But sometimes it must be done in order to remove the distortions which increase Sin if, by the persistence of wrong thoughts, they produce wrong ways of living.

It is possible however to conquer the dangers implied in concentrating on Sin if we look at it not directly, but in the light of what enables us to resist it—reunion overcoming estrangement. Sin is the name for the act in which we turn away from the participation in the divine ground from which we come and to which we go. Sin is the turning toward ourselves, making ourselves the center of our world and of ourselves. Sin is the drive in everyone, even the most self-restraining one, to draw as much as possible of the world into oneself. But we can be fully aware of this only if we have found a point above ourselves. Whoever has found himself after he had lost himself knows how deep his self-loss was. If we look at our estrangement from a point of reunion, we are no longer in danger of brooding over our estrangement. We can speak of Sin, because its power over us is broken.

It is certainly not broken by ourselves. The attempt to break the power of Sin by the power of good will has been described by Paul as the attempt to fulfill the law, the law in our mind, in our inmost self, which is the law of God. The end of this attempt is failure, guilt, and despair. The law with its commands and prohibitions, in spite of its function to reveal and restrict evil, also provokes resistance against itself. In a language both poetic and profoundly psychological, Paul says that the sin which dwells in our members is asleep until the moment in which it is awakened by the "thou shalt not." Sin uses the commandments in order to become alive. Prohibition awakens sleeping desire. It arouses the power and consciousness of Sin, but cannot break its power. Only if we accept with our whole being the message that it *is* broken, is it also broken in us.

This picture of Sin is a picture full of ugliness, suffering, and shame and, at the same time, full of drama and passion. It is the picture of us as the battleground of powers greater than we. It does not show a division of men into black and white, into bad ones and good ones. It does not look like the threatening finger of an authority urging us: Do not sin! But it is the vision of something infinitely important, happening on this small planet, in our bodies and our minds. It raises mankind to the place in the universe where decisive things happen in every moment, decisive for the ultimate meaning of all existence. In each of us such decisions occur *in* us and *through* us. This is our burden; this is our despair. This is our greatness.

5

GRIEF, DEATH,
AND THE ETERNAL

The Christian and Grief

By *Granger E. Westberg*
Institute of Religion, Houston, Texas

> *Grieve not as those who have no hope.*
> —I Thessalonians 4:13

The question is often asked, Is it right for a Christian person to grieve? Or, How should a Christian person respond to the loss of something or someone very dear to him?

There are eight words in the Scripture (I Thess. 4:13) which are often misunderstood. "Grieve not as those who have no hope." As we have grown up in the Church I am sure that many of us have felt that we were taught that when a truly Christian person confronts a grief situation he ought not to grieve. It is as if we took these eight words and cut them down to two so that all we have left is an admonition, Grieve not.

But this is certainly out of character with the stories of people found on the pages of Holy Scripture. As we look at both the Old Testament and the New Testament we find that strong men, brave men, the great leaders of the faith through the centuries, grieved, sorrowed, shed tears when there was cause to grieve and to sorrow. The Psalmist says, "My tears have been my food day and night."

When we speak of grief we usually think of the loss of a loved one through death. And I certainly mean to include grief related to death. But I would like also to include other forms of grief of which there are so many. We all go through periods of grief whenever we lose anything or any person very important to us. And this loss does not always occur through death.

For instance, one of the more common grief situations arises out of our mobile culture due to change of employment or promotions where families are uprooted so often that one out of five Americans moves every year. And this uprooting cuts the family off from relationships in the community which the children and parents have such need for. Every member of the family is affected in some way as they are separated from people and things which have grown dear to them. Perhaps we ought to question whether corporations which transfer their key employees every two to five years are doing a wise thing. Here is a family who were transferred for the third time in seven years. Now they have lived in the present town for two years, and their children after some difficulty have finally found themselves in relation to their playmates and their school. The company now "invites" him to move for the fourth time. The mother in this family says that they have never before felt such a sense of belonging as they have in this town, and they had hoped they could stay there for a long, long time. But her husband is on his way to a vice-presidency, and the corporation operates on the assumption that it is good for its men to move frequently. I am not so sure. We who work in the field of religion and medicine see a great many sick or upset people in close relation to an uprooting experience. I see children who are thrown into turmoil three months before the move and for three or more months after the move. Certainly such practices contribute to the instability of our society, and corporations would do well to take a new look at the long-term results of such constant moving.

Or let us think of the problem of divorce. Certainly divorce is a situation which creates grief in the hearts of those who have now lost someone who once was dear to them. It is almost like a living death to see the one whom you still love turning his back on you, figuratively slapping you in the face.

Another form of grief may be retirement. Not all people look forward to the arbitrary retirement age of sixty-five.

They feel that they are good for at least another ten years. They hope the company they work for will make an exception in their case. But when their sixty-fifth birthday comes, they too receive the summons. And many of these people leave their jobs with a heavy heart, having lost all reason for living.

Or we think of a man in his forties or fifties who is laid off indefinitely because of a business recession. Or the person who has worked diligently to gain advancement in his job who has worked overtime and weekends to demonstrate his ability to take over a particular situation. Finally that job is open, and he is sure that he will be chosen. But the boss brings in his nephew to take over. A cause for grief? Of course it is!

Or the loss of a child, not through death but through marriage. The child moves away, and now the house is lifeless. A house once filled with laughter and joy is now as quiet as a tomb. Or the loss of a child who has turned against his mother and father and lives his life in a manner completely contrary to their teaching. Or the loss of health, the loss of a limb, the loss of eyesight or hearing. Loss of a home through fire or tornado. Any of these things sets in motion a cycle of grief.

In some families grief comes with the loss of a pet who has been a part of everything that has gone on in that household for ten years or more. Grief is a natural part of human experience. We face minor grief almost daily in some situation or another. To say that a Christian does not grieve is not only totally unrealistic but is also incompatible with the whole Christian message.

The one Bible verse that every school child knows by heart is the two-word verse "Jesus wept." These words describe a man who, when grief came, was able to weep. No. When we say, "Grieve not," we imply that we are to be Stoics like the Greeks of old. But we are Christians, not Stoics, and in our Scriptures we see grief as normal and potentially creative. So I would like to suggest that in this eight-word portion of the Scripture we put a comma after the first word, so that it now reads, "Grieve, not as those who have no hope"—but for goodness sake, grieve.

The minister sees people in a variety of situations related to sorrow. In our ministry to people in sorrow we sense that people tend to follow a pattern—a pattern which includes perhaps ten stages. We also sense that a person who is able to go through these stages, accept them as a rugged school of life, a kind of refiner's fire, and believe that God lives and is personally concerned about him throughout such an experience—this person comes through grief a stronger person, a deeper person, and a person better able to help others who are grieving. While he is going through his grief, he questions the value of his faith; he questions everything about his former religious convictions. But if somehow he is able to maintain his relationship with God through regular worship and through fellowship with the concerned community of believers, he does come through his grief a stronger person. Like Job of old, he is beset on all sides but he refuses to give up his basic faith. He says, "I know that my Redeemer liveth." Whatever comes, he will still believe that God lives. All through the centuries, people who have been able to face grief in the knowledge that God still cares about them say that grief can be counted among the great deepening experiences of life.

These ten stages of grief I would like to describe as very normal. In effect, the theme of this sermon is "good grief." This is what we are talking about today—good grief as opposed to "unhealthy" or "bad" grief. Grief can be creative and productive, provided we move through it with the help of our faith and the supporting concern of those around us. However, if we spend too much time in any one of the stages, it could be bad grief and it could be unhealthy.

Let us look at these ten stages.

The first stage is shock. God has so made us that we can take pain and sorrow and even tragedy and somehow we are able to bear it. When the sorrow is overwhelming, we are temporarily anesthetized in response to the experience. We are grateful for this anesthesia, for it keeps us from having to face the problem all at once. This shock stage—or perhaps it should be called a countershock—may last anywhere from a few minutes to a few hours to a few days. If it goes on for many weeks, then it probably is unhealthy. But don't be afraid of the shock in the early stages of grief. Sometimes at the funeral parlor we greet the sorrowing wife and find that she is almost radiant, as if nothing had happened. Everyone says, "What tremendous faith she has." You see we always tend to equate faith with a stoical spirit, not with tears. This woman probably is experiencing a temporary anesthesia helping her over the hump until she is ready for the second stage, which is *emotional release.*

This is the time when it begins to dawn on us how terrible this loss is. Then the flood gates are forced open by tremendous emotional surging within us. We are almost uncontrollable in the expression of our grief. But we have been given tear glands to use. And we are supposed to use them when we have reason to use them.

In our society it is very difficult for men to cry because we have been taught as little tots that boys do not cry. When we fell and skinned our knee, someone picked us up and said, "Ah, ah, boys don't cry." And when we were eight years old and hurt ourselves we did not dare to cry, nor at eighteen when something happened about which we ought to have cried; and at thirty-eight when some great loss hit us, we could not cry. A typical man thinks that crying is not only a sign of weakness, but he is sure if he ever lets himself go emotionally this will be the end of him. But this is not true. It is the person who holds himself tense, who refuses to let go, who is in for trouble. The Scriptures will bear us out that when great calamities came to men of faith, they cried. (Now to the ladies present, we perhaps do not need to encourage you. We say to you, "Let's not overdo a good thing.)

The third stage is a feeling of utter depression and isolation. It is as if God is no longer in his heaven, as if God does not care. And it is during these days that we are sure that no one else has ever grieved exactly as we are grieving. And it is true that no one has ever grieved exactly as we are grieving. But the awful experience of being utterly depressed and isolated is a universal phenomenon. When we find ourselves down in the depths of despair, as some of us may be even today, know that we are saying that even this is normal. This too shall pass. One way to describe a depression is that it is much like a very dark day when the clouds have so blacked out the sun that everyone says, "The sun isn't shining today." Now you and I know that the sun is shining. But it appears as if it is not, and even the automobiles have to have their headlights on. Perhaps you have had occasion to make an airplane trip on a day like that. Your plane climbs up and up through these layers of heavy dark clouds and then finally you get upon top at 18,000 or even 28,000 feet, and the sun suddenly pours through the windows of the plane and you look out and see the white billowy clouds which are so black on the other side. People exclaim, "Isn't it beautiful!" Then someone says, "Too bad the people downstairs can't see this." But the people downstairs are saying, "The sun isn't shining today." The sun is shining. But something has come between the people and the sun. This is what a depression is, a sense of isolation. We say God does not care. We even say there is no God. Many people in Scripture have said the same thing. "Why art thou cast down, O my soul? My soul is cast down within me. I say to God my Rock, why hast thou forgotten me? My adversaries taunt me. They say, 'Where is your God?'"

Deep inside it is as if we are saying on those days, "Where is my God?" Jesus himself faced this loneliness when on the cross he cried out, "My God, my God, why hast thou forsaken me?"

The fourth stage is the stage of physical symptoms of distress. Working as I do in a medical center, I see a great many people who are ill in close relationship to an unresolved grief situation. It seems that these people have become ill because they have not been able to work through their grief for some reason. They are stopped at one of the points in the ten-stage process. And unless something is done to extricate them from this situation, they may stay ill. The situation is often something like this. Let me give you a composite picture of some of the people we meet in the hospital.

Here is a young couple in their early thirties, Mr. and Mrs. B., who live in a small town in Illinois or Indiana or Iowa. They live in a lovely little home there, and he works at a job he likes very much. He does not make too much money, but he comes home every noon for lunch, and they putter in the garden together, and he is home every day at 5:00. Life is rich in this community. They both were born and raised there. They have their families there. They happen not to have any children, but their nieces and nephews are in and out of the house all the time, and so they lack for nothing. Then one day Mr. B. goes to a convention in Chicago and there he meets a businessman who sees potential in this young fellow and invites Mr. B. to join his business firm, offering him a salary three times what he is making in Iowa. And so he accepts the job, of course, because in America if you get an offer to make more money, you take it. Everyone who knows this couple is proud of them because they have made good. So they move to a suburb of Chicago, buy a lovely home, and everything is just as it is supposed to be in the storybooks. But Mr. B. does not come home for lunch anymore, and his wife misses him very much. After a week or two he finds that he often has to stay downtown for dinner to entertain customers. After a few weeks he is so well thought of that they send him out on the road, and now he is gone Tuesday, Wednesday, and Thursday of every week. All she has to do is to face the four walls of this beautiful home. She is not an outgoing type of person, and she has never had to make her own friends. Her beautiful home begins to look like a prison to her, and she begins to resent what this new job has done to her in taking her husband from her. She resents her husband for always putting his business first. No longer is she the center of his life. So she begins to grieve, much as she would if he had died. She does not dare tell anyone about this, because this is foolish. After all, she is supposed to be very happy about this promotion to a new and better way of living.

But she finds herself engulfed by loneliness, a sense of isolation and depression. Then she begins to develop physical symptoms of distress—headaches and backaches and all kinds of aches. Finally she tells her husband, and he insists that she see a doctor. The doctor gives her some medications, and she feels better for a time. But after a bit she has a recurrence of these same symptoms. The doctor says, "I think you had better come into the hospital for a complete check-up." And she does. But they find nothing physically wrong with her. But she is still sick—just as sick as a person with something like a broken leg or an ulcer. Then the doctor talks with a chaplain and asks him to look in on Mrs. B. because he thinks this illness is related to some family problems. So the minister stops in. At first Mrs. B. talks only about pleasant matters, but if she finds the chaplain to be understanding and easy to talk to and not in a hurry, then often a typical Mrs. B. will haltingly tell the whole story of her resentment which is related to the loss of her husband and everything that was dear to her back in Iowa. Then she breaks down and tells how she really feels, and how she hates her husband's business firm, how she hates everything about this move. Her hostility, her feelings of guilt, all these things are intertwined with her grief. This is one of the reasons she is ill. Here is where the doctor and the minister must work together to help her to understand the cause of these physical symptoms and to help her to work through these as one who is now going through a growing-up experience, which in her case didn't happen to take place at the usual age of eighteen or twenty. It is a delayed reaction. But if she isn't helped to understand this, she may stop at this stage and remain ill for a long time.

The fifth stage is when we find ourselves constantly preoccupied with the loss. Now we really get worried. When we are asked a question we often reply "What was that? Excuse me, what did you say?" We just can't concentrate. The loss is all we can think about. Now we feel that something is happening to our mind. But this too is normal. This is one of the reasons I feel it's helpful for us to talk to each other in advance about the feelings that happen to all of us in grief. It is the panic of thinking that we are going through something abnormal that throws us deeper into despair.

The sixth stage is when we develop a sense of guilt about the loss. Certainly if we lose a loved one through death, all of us need to feel guilty about some of the things we didn't do for this person when he was alive, or the things that we did do to this person when he was alive. To try to put these thoughts out of mind entirely without talking them over with someone could be unhealthy. Contrite confession of real guilt is a part of every Sunday morning worship service. We all need to say, "Have mercy upon me, O God, according to the multitude of thy tender mercies; blot out my transgressions. For I know my transgressions and my sin is ever before me." Dealing realistically with guilt is a necessary part of the grief process.

The seventh stage is one of hostility and resentment. Now we are able to express some of the strong feelings we have been holding back. We are gradually moving up out of the depression. We find ourselves very critical of everything and everybody who is related to the loss. If it was a death, we express hostility toward anyone who cared for the patient. We are hostile to the doctor because he operated. Or we are hostile to the doctor because he did not operate. And no matter what he had done, it would have been wrong. If we talk to the minister and he encourages us to say what we really think, then one day we may say, "Why did God do this to me? How can He be a God of love if He treats people like this?" With Carlyle we impatiently cry, "God sits in his heaven and does nothing."

The eighth stage is inability to return to usual activities. Now we try in every way to go back to the usual activities that we have been engaged in. We feel much more like our former self, yet something holds us back. We just cannot seem to resume our normal activities. Why is this? Well, I'm sure there are many reasons, but among them is the fact that our American way of life makes it so difficult for us to grieve in the presence of other people that we have to carry all the grief within ourselves. Do you remember when we were children people could grieve more openly? The men wore black armbands, and the women wore black veils for six months to a year; so everyone was reminded daily of their loss. One of the last public personages to wear a black armband was President Franklin Roosevelt at the death of his mother. The children who saw pictures of him would ask, "Why is he wearing that black armband?" In Europe they still wear some symbol of grieving for six months to a year. But we have somehow got the impression that grief is out of place in civilized society. We frown on grieving and especially when it is public. So we offer our sympathy to our grieving friends once after their loss has occurred, and from then on we say, "Let's get back to business as usual again."

Suppose you and your wife are with a widow whose husband died a year or so ago. As the three of you talk together you recall a very humorous story her husband once told you. You are about to tell it, and then you think, "Oh, no. No. I must not reopen this wound. I must be considerate of her. I should not mention him." And so you carefully steer away from it. But the reverse is true. Actually if you told this story, you would see her laugh and enjoy it. Then you might see a tear or two. If you were to say, "I'm sorry, I shouldn't have told that story," her response would in all probability be, "Shouldn't have told it. You're the first person in months who has even mentioned my husband. No one ever talks about him anymore. It is a wonderful feeling to know that someone still remembers him." Now is not this a part of the task of the Church, the community of the concerned as we'd like to call it, that we show concern for one another and particularly when one has suffered a great loss? "Therefore bear ye one another's burdens."

Number nine is a gradual awareness of the unreality of our present attitude. How gradually this awareness comes depends both on the inner strength we have and with the intensity of the loss. This awareness comes in small bits with the passing of time and to the extent to which our faith in the constancy of God is renewed. Now and then we get a little glimpse of hope in one experience or another. This cloud which had been so dark begins to break up, and rays of light come through. We may be in deep grief anywhere from a few months to two or three years. We are never quite sure how long grief is going to last. If it goes much beyond two years, perhaps we ought to get some special help.

Gradually we realize that our present attitude of shutting out all new opportunities for meaningful living is unrealistic. We find that other experiences in life can be meaningful again.

In Rabbi Joshua Liebman's book, *Peace of Mind*, there is a chapter on "Grief's Slow Wisdom" in which the rabbi tells the story of a woman who for many years after her musician husband died locked up the piano he had used and kept everything in the room just exactly as he had left it. (This chapter is based on the Talmud and on the studies of Dr. Erich Lindemann of Harvard in connection with the Boston Coconut Grove fire.) She locked the keyboard of the piano because no one else was to have the right to play that piano again. It was as if she had locked the keyboard of her own life allowing no one else ever to play a melody on the piano of her life. Well, of course, no one else will ever play the same melody, but do not lock the keyboard. Allow other melodies to be played, and many of them will enrich our lives. But do not lock the keyboard.

Finally, number ten is readjustment to reality. Number ten is not "We become our old selves again." When we go through any grief experience, we are different people from then on. If we go through it believing essentially throughout the experience that God is with us, despite the prevalence of disturbing doubts, we come through the experience with a different quality of faith than we had before. We are stronger, our thoughts go deeper, and we are better able to help our neighbor through experiences similar to the one through which we have just passed.

This then is a very brief description of the ten stages of good grief. First shock, then emotional release, depression and isolation, physical symptoms of distress, constant preoccupation with the loss, sense of guilt, hostility and resentment, inability to return to usual activities, gradual awareness of the unreality of present attitudes, and, finally, readjustment to reality.

Such an experience reminds us of the psalm "Yea though I walk through the valley of the shadow of death, I will fear no evil, for thou art with me." Or another psalm, "I waited patiently for the Lord. And he did incline unto my cry. He drew me up out of the desolate pit, and he put a new song in my mouth. Blessed is he who puts his trust in the Lord."

So we say, "Grieve—not as those who have no hope," but grieve.

The Work of Our Hands:
Three Responses to the Crisis of Death

By J. Coert Rylaarsdam
The University of Chicago

The last Sunday of October is Memorial Sunday at the University of Chicago. It is at this time that we pay tribute to university colleagues who have departed this life during the past year; we think of their achievements and honor their memory. Our university day of special remembrance is set in the context of the Christian Feast of All Saints, a fact that invites us to ponder the import of the struggle of life in the context of the meaning and mystery of death.

The first lesson this morning consisted of the Ninetieth Psalm. I want to repeat small parts of both the preface and conclusion of that psalm. First from the preface: "O Lord, thou hast been our dwelling place in all generations. Before the mountains were brought forth, or ever thou hadst formed the earth and the world, even from everlasting to everlasting, thou art God." And from the conclusion: "Let the favor of the Lord our God be upon us, and establish thou the work of our hands upon us. Yea, the work of our hands establish thou it." The preface talks about the eternity and centrality of God; the conclusion alludes to the human struggle and to the inability of man to bring it to completion.

This majestic preface and this solemn conclusion provide a setting for the main part of the psalm in which the poet offers a very realistic appraisal of the struggle of his own life. The storms of life were very thick and very harsh for this

man. The irrational factors in his situation baffled him; "we
are consumed by thine anger." The hurdles were getting higher
all the time, and things were not coming out as he had hoped
they would. So much of life was no longer amenable to plan-
ning. It was impossible to manage anything fully, and there was
so much in the situation that was utterly irretrievable. Possibilities that had once beckoned no longer offered themselves.
The brutishness of life was now in his experience being over-
taken by an awareness of its brevity; time was running out.
"Three score years and ten, or, by reason of great strength, four-
score; yet is their burden but labour and sorrow, and we soon
fly away." His powers are failing. At night he cannot study as late
as he used to. His work is incomplete, his goal unattained, and
he is frustrated.

The main part of the psalm relates the old pilgrim's
"moment of truth." It reminds us of a line in Thomas Gray's
"Elegy": "The paths of glory lead but to the grave." The old
psalmist is frustrated because he cannot build his world as he
had hoped and planned. The walls of the city of man remain
unfinished. There is no doubt about his vocation to build that
city. For this ancient psalmist, "the city of man" was the will of
God. It was a divine commandment that he should build it. It is
precisely this deep awareness of a sense of impossible vocation
that frustrates him. Unless God comes to his rescue in the
building of the city, it will never be finished. That brings on the
prayer in the conclusion, "The work of our hands establish thou
it." In the hour of his frustration the pilgrim of life who lays
bare his experience in the Ninetieth Psalm does not ask for a
change of assignment; he does not deny the importance of what
he finds it impossible to complete. For him the city of man is still
the will of God. That is the key to his faith, as well as the reason
for his need of it. He does not ask God to rescue him from a
hard life; he asks him to help him in it because he never doubts
that accomplishment in this life is important.

The psalmist believed in the importance of man's life
and work in this world. That is important for us who use his lines
at this memorial service. At this service we honor our colleagues
claimed by death: trustees, faculty, staff, students. We honor

men and women—all of whom were, in one way or another, dedicated to the life and work of the university. We honor their accomplishments. We prize their legacy. And we dedicate ourselves to their example because, with the psalmist, we share the hopes that were also the occasions of their frustration.

The men and women we honor belonged to the university; that is, they *all* assumed the importance of man's life and action in this world. They all believed that man's plans, visions, and effort played a part in the realization of the meaning of his life. They did not all believe in God in the way the psalmist did. Some of them would probably have been offended at the thought of calling upon God as the psalmist did, to ask him to step in and take over when their own powers faltered. Some of them would have insisted that men only "have each other" and that the notion of God must be limited to the resources in human continuity; others would have shared the biblical faith that human purpose and design are only a reflection of a much larger purpose, the purpose of the living God in whose "image" man is created. But however they may have differed in that respect, they all believed in the city of man and its meaning. It is for that that we honor them and remember them in this chapel today.

To be sure, the psalmist is a "theist"; he invokes the power and goodness of God: "Establish thou the work of our hands upon us. Yea, the work of our hands establish thou it." But he does so to establish the city of man and its meaning, not to displace it. If in this service we pointed to God and what he does or can do in such a way as to discount or deny the meaning of the city of man, we would not really honor the memory of our fallen comrades in the life and program of our university; in a sense, we would mock it, however unintentionally. It is important to stress this, for Christian faith and witness have often forgotten it. It is unfortunately true that the noblest of men and women, people who are unselfishly dedicated to the building of the city of man, are suspicious of the Christian faithful and dread the very thought of being "remembered" in a service at a Christian altar. If Christians would, indeed, honor all men who dedicated their lives to truth and goodness, they would confess with the psalmist that God the Redeemer is no other than God the Creator "who hast been our dwelling place in all generations." For the psalmist, redemption is the disclosure of the meaning of creation, not its abrogation.

In a singular way, the university is the epitome of the city of man. Perhaps the United Nations building in New York City is its nearest rival as a symbol of man's effort to find meaning and significance for his life by means of his own power and intelligence. At the university we are dedicated to the understanding of man's life in terms of what it is in itself, and in terms of what its possibilities are. We are dedicated to the exploitation of the world in which we live—physical, social, economic, and so on—so that we may use it to help realize the possibilities of human life as we find them. A university is not primarily interested in the production of goods just for the sake of producing them, but for the sake of realizing the fullness of the life of man. The community of learning is dedicated to exhibit the fullness of the measure of manhood, to realize the meaning of the spirit of man in his dignity and possibility.

The motto inscribed on the seal of this university sums up this burden of the human quest: "Crescat scientia; vita excolatur." In our university hymn we recall the "White City" that stood here for a year or two; and then we sing about "the city gray that never more shall die." These gray stone buildings—ever growing in number, and perpetually being renovated and remodeled—set forth man's never-ending quest for meaning and for the realization of a goal and a hope. New horizons are superimposed upon new horizons in this pilgrimage toward the humanization of life and the attainment of human possibility. And in this the university exalts the human act and the time, space, and matter by means of which it accomplishes its work. The psalmist had also worked with these elements; he had found time fleeting, and space and matter were recalcitrant. But he persisted even amid despair, for he was convinced of the meaningfulness of the human act and the human struggle. This, too, is the basis and focus for life and work in the university.

In a profound sense the university is the product of the biblical spirit enshrined in the Ninetieth Psalm. This is a matter of great surprise, for there were no universities in ancient Jerusalem. The analytical methods of science were developed in Greece rather than in Israel. The study of man and his possibilities as an end in itself was a preoccupation of Athens; Israel simply inferred its understanding of man from the faith about God it proclaimed. Nevertheless, Israel played a profoundly motivating role in making men persist in the human quest epitomized by the university.

What Israel said in its confession of God was that he, too, had plans, a hope, and a kingdom as his goal—that he, too, used time, space, and matter as the means for the realization of his goal. This was meant by the announcement, "The earth is the Lord's and the fullness thereof"; the reality men call God uses the world purposively, as man does. That is what the Bible means when it calls God "creator of heaven and earth"; he uses it all. Creation is not a species of natural history, but a confession of faith about the meaning of nature. If we take this biblical notion of creation seriously, we learn that in our manipulation and use of our world and its possibilities we are handling the very forces which ancient Israel said were used by the living God. We find ourselves, in our science and learning, in a situation where we are co-workers with God and where life is holy.

In the story of creation we are told that God said, "Let us make man in our own image, and let him have dominion." This is the biblical franchise for the university and, indeed, for all human efforts at the realization of the possibilities potential in man's life. Biblical faith is a this-worldly faith, notably in its Jewish version. The so-called material quality of Western civilization is something it comes by quite honestly; it is derived from the Bible. It is interested in making time, space, and matter serve man in the realization of the meaning of his life, both because this makes man human and, in the biblical tradition, because this makes him a co-worker with the transcendent reality of God. In the Western world the kingdom of God and the city of man really belong together. Life is holy; the common life in the university, in the professions, the shop, and the home. God and man use the same world.

Death was serious for the author of Psalm Ninety. It was serious because it set a limit to the possibility of meaningful activity as far as he was concerned: "Three score years and ten . . . and they soon fly away." Death is a serious thing in a humanistic community such as that of the university. It is serious precisely because a community such as this attaches very great importance to the results of human action, discovery, and achievement. There are traditions in which death is incidental. Where time and process represent a transiency without meaning, where temporal existence is conceived as a matter of inescapably meaningless suffering, where the struggle of life is assumed to be foredoomed to sterility—there death is either incidental or, better yet, a blessed release. But if, as we say, we live in a world where the meaning of our existence is disclosed and where, by our effort, we also participate in its discovery— the common confession of humanists, Jews, and Christians— there the fact of death constitutes a tremendous crisis and challenge. The critical decisiveness of death can, indeed, be measured by the relative importance we attach to the city of man. Is the battle of life worthwhile after all, given this fact of death? That was the psalmist's question, and it is ours. Does our effort really matter? Does it count? And, if it does, how does it count? I want to refer to three ways in which the Bible deals with this challenge posed by the fact of death.

For the first way, we look at the account of the death of the patriarch Isaac in the Book of Genesis. It says, "And Isaac breathed his last; and he died, and was gathered to his fathers, old and full of days." The very tenor of the words makes it clear that the death of Isaac represented no crisis. The challenge of that crisis had been met. Isaac belonged to a people. Though he was "old and full of days" at the end, none of the causes and goals for which he had toiled in his lifetime had come to their completion. But that was not a calamity, for they were the causes and goals of the entire people. The death of Isaac did not mean the death of his hopes; others entered into his place to undertake his burdens and further the cause. Despite his death, Isaac's hopes were alive. There was a corporate character about the human family that made this possible; the Book of Genesis always speaks of the final reality as "the God of the fathers."

This consciousness of our corporate human existence as a way of dealing with the crisis for the city of man occasioned by death is by no means denuded of its validity and power. This is especially true in the Jewish community. One of the men we remember at this service is Jason Aronson, a young man of great ability and high purpose who was taken away in the early summer of his years. I was deeply moved when I read the address given by Professor Strauss at Mr. Aronson's funeral. He recalled that during the last three weeks of Mr. Aronson's life they had read the Bible together. What had filled the young scholar's mind ever more during those last weeks was the humble and conscious awareness of the fact that he belonged to an *am olam*, that he was a member of an eternal people. What brought him poise and peace was the fact that he was a son of the Covenant and that all he valued and had worked for would live on and be served by the community. And so it is. Sons of the Covenant, members of the Body of Christ, children of the family of man. These corporate connections, illustrated by the story of Isaac, can perhaps not bear all the challenge created for the city of man by the crisis of death; nevertheless, without them the crisis is never fully borne; our age of individualism has rediscovered that.

The second way in which the Bible deals with the crisis is best illustrated by Psalm Ninety. The author also belonged to a people. There is no evidence that he had been ostracized by the community of the Covenant or that he had forcibly uprooted himself from it. Yet it seems not to have given him any comfort or served as a resource. His experience reminds us of men today; men have often forgotten the purposes of their allegiances. They find it hard to remember that the ends of their lives and the ends of the communities with which they identify are the same, or ought to be. As the Psalmist looked around he saw that so much besides his own powers lay in ruins. The mourning for his own death would become a part of the symphony of the mourning for Jerusalem. How could a community as battered as he was himself provide help? He appeals to the Creative Source of life itself, his own and that of the community, "Establish thou the work of our hands; yea, the work of our hands, establish thou it." He finds rest and peace in his prayer. Life is one and God is one; he who brings death also brings life. He lives by the faith that the meaning of his life will not be lost, even though he has no idea how it will be saved. Waiting, hoping, enduring. For God is man's home in all generations, and he will in his own way establish the meaning of the city of man.

The third way in which the Bible deals with the crisis is characteristic of the New Testament. To deal with the crisis for the city of man posed by the fact of death, it appeals to the city of God. What is the central thrust of faith in the Jewish tradition is that God is the lord of history, the one who establishes man's purposes, and his own, in this world. God uses even the tyrants to serve his purposes. Alongside this is the thrust of the New Testament which says that he uses death as well. The significance and meaning of man's goals are transformed by God through it; the end no longer lies in time. But the meaning of what is attempted in time is not lost; the city of man is transfigured and taken up into the city of God. "In his will is our peace" is the word that sums up this meeting of the crisis; the purpose of life is realized as much, or even more, because of death than in spite of it in this third theme. While at its worst, this facet of biblical thought can lead to an abominable historical irresponsibility, at its best it can make men both heroic and triumphant. "For I am persuaded that neither death nor life, nor angels nor principalities, nor things present nor things to come, nor height nor depth, nor anything else in all creation will be able to separate us from the love of God in Christ Jesus."

These three ways in which the Bible deals with the challenge faced by the fact of death are not mutually exclusive. They interweave; now one, now the other, is in the ascendency. We do not have to choose one; we can respond to one, to two, or to three as we receive grace to make response. We may be carried by the fact that we belong to an "eternal people"; we can find rest in the hope that the city of man will be built as the city of man, or that its intention will be transfigured by the city of God. But in any case, the crisis will have been dissolved in the life that is all in all.

The Appearances of Our Risen Lord

By W. B. Blakemore
The University of Chicago

I have chosen to speak with you this morning regarding the Gospel passages which deal with the appearances of the risen Lord as reported to have occurred in a forty-day period between Easter Day and an ascension in glory into heaven. I undertake this discussion with very great trepidation and with the expectation that many of you may find the presentation quite unsatisfactory. Some of you may feel that I make too much of these reports of the risen Lord; others of you may feel that I hedge too much in what I say and that I am wobbly in the faith. My only refuge in that regard is to say that as a Christian minister it is hardly my purpose to satisfy you or to please you but only to see what I can honestly say about these passages. Also I must, as a Christian minister, honestly admit that confronted by them I have all sorts of intellectual difficulties, doubts, skepticisms, and may produce more confusion than clarification.

Let us briefly recapitulate the biblical record.

The Gospel of Mark reports the resurrection morning only in terms of an empty tomb and the promise that Jesus will meet his disciples in Galilee. Originally this Gospel seems to have included no report of an appearance of the risen Christ. However, some very early appendixes to the gospel report an appearance to Mary Magdalene, a second appearance in "another form," whatever those words may mean, to two of the disciples, and a final appearance to the eleven gathered at a meal after which the Lord ascended into heaven.

The Gospel of Matthew reports an appearance, evidently on Easter Day, to Mary Magdalene and the other Mary, and a subsequent appearance on the mountainside to the eleven disciples.

The Gospel according to Luke reports that two disciples walking on a road some seven miles from Jerusalem were joined by a stranger who accompanied them into the village of Emmaus, where they partook of a meal together. In this breaking of bread the disciples realized that the stranger was the risen Christ. Later they reported the incident to the eleven disciples gathered in a room. As they made their report, the risen Lord joined the company, and again as he ate in their midst, all were convinced of his presence with them.

According to the Gospel of John, the Lord appeared first to Mary Magdalene on the resurrection day and later that same day to the disciples, gathered together, but without Thomas. When told of the appearance, Thomas doubted it, but some eight days later when the eleven were all together, the Lord again appeared, and Thomas, seeing and feeling the wounds of the crucifixion, believed. Finally the Lord appeared again to his disciples on the Sea of Tiberias in the early morning. Here he ate with them and especially charged Peter with the responsibility of feeding the Lord's sheep.

In his first letter to the Corinthians, Paul reports some six appearances, including his own vision of the risen Lord at the time Paul was brought to conversion in the dramatic experience outside Damascus.

It is difficult to get a firm count of the number of different times the Christ is said to have appeared; it is somewhere between nine and twelve. It is also difficult to count the number of people to whom he appeared—five hundred or more when we include Paul's statement that on one occasion he did appear to five hundred.

What shall we do with these Gospel accounts?

There is one level at which these reports may be interpreted without any great intellectual difficulty. One can accept them as parables of the moral life. The appearance of the Lord at the Sea of Tiberias can be accepted as a parable of charitable concern and Christian ministry. The disciples had been fishing all night without success. The Lord appeared on the shore, and learning that the disciples had caught nothing, he said, "Cast the net on the right side of the boat"; or as the New English Bible states it, "Shoot the net to starboard." They shot the net to starboard and made a great catch from which they breakfasted on the shore. Then the Lord turned to Peter and three times gave him the serious charge, "Feed my sheep." This can be taken as a figure that we should have concern for each other and serve each other. Certainly that is a valid moral drawn from the incident.

Or consider the incident of the men walking toward Emmaus. Eventually they sat down to a meal with the stranger who had appeared at their side. In the fullness of sharing together the very goods of this life they entered into a fellowship rich enough for them to know and recognize each other. One can moralize this incident also, and the moral is valid: only in the fullest and richest sharing of life with our fellowman do we truly discover our fellowman and ourselves. It is around a table, eating together, whether it be sharing the joys of a feast, sharing the gratitude for harvest, sharing the meagerness of a crust, or even sharing the disaster of famine, it is in sharing in common that we come to know our fellow for who he is and he knows us.

Even the incident of the doubting Thomas can be taken in this moralistic way. Indeed the Lord, is reported to have himself made it the occasion for a moral comment, saying to Thomas, "Have you believed because you have seen me? Blessed are those who have not seen and yet believed."

But somehow we recognize that to go no further with these reports of the appearances than to treat them as moral parables is to cheat at the religious level. In order to present the values of charitable ministry, full fellowship, and firm faith, one hardly needs to tell stories of post-resurrection appearances; something much more must be intended by these reports. But when we push on to this something more, we strike

200 W. B. Blakemore

levels at which these accounts become an embarrassment to the modern mind.

These passages are today rarely preached about. The habit in all our churches is that we make a great deal of the earthly life of Jesus of Nazareth. We intensify our interest in him during the Lenten period preceding Easter, and we bring our concern and preoccupation to a grand climax on Easter morning. We acknowledge the Resurrection in a general way, but then we bring the season to a very quick close. The Sunday after Easter is even sometimes called Low Sunday, and the contemporary church, which has made much of the forty days of Lent preceding Easter, ignores the analogous forty days after Easter, which really ought to get more attention because they were presumably the days in which the confirmation of the Resurrection took place by virtue of the appearances of the Lord. But the very idea of these appearances has become a stumbling block and an embarrassment.

Oddly this situation is the reverse of what prevailed in the early days of the church. So far as we can tell, the early Christians were not embarrassed by the idea that their Lord should have appeared in some form after his crucifixion; what embarrassed them was that he had been crucified, that his manner of death identified him with the lowest and most despised elements of society. Wherever they tried to tell the Gospel story in the ancient world, the cross was a stumbling block; the mention of crucifixion was repugnant and repulsive; ideational associations were such that one who had been crucified could only be identified with murderers and robbers and brigands and men of lowest passions.

For the man of today, crucifixion is in no way part of his ordinary experience. The only associations which the cross has are its religious associations. It is now a glorious symbol, and we have to work at it to remind ourselves of the kind of death it meant or even to remind ourselves that it meant death. Jesus' crucifixion is no stumbling block for us because we have become all too familiar with the unjust execution of innocent men and women. Jesus' crucifixion is easily accepted religiously, not by our overcoming a resistance to acknowledge a criminal as Lord, but because we look upon him rather as the first of martyrs going nobly to a death he did not deserve. Indeed, so much of our religious understanding can be summarized and borne by the figure of the crucified Jesus that we are prone to be too easily satisfied with going no further. Jesus then, became the figure of our highest manhood, going to his death on principle, out of love and affection for his fellowman. He becomes the symbol of sacrificial love, the emblem of all those forms of service which do not count the cost. He becomes heroic in stature, accepting the injustice of this world without complaint. Toward this crucified Christ vast portions of our natural reverence may rightfully flow. But if it is only in these terms that we accept Christianity, then we might with all propriety substitute many another hero of the race, for we are exalting a quality widely present in mankind: the quality of devotion to family shown by a father; a mother's complete submission to the needs of a child; a daughter's care for aging parents; a man's service to his community, devotion to work, risks taken for the advancement of knowledge, and so on. A humanist religion can well accept the crucified Jesus as its emblem, or as has frequently been suggested, it can substitute Socrates drinking the hemlock. Socrates was unjustly condemned to death; he assured that no debt would be left behind to impeach his dignity; he honestly voiced what a later age would call agnosticism. He, too, is worthy of great veneration.

The kind of appreciation of our humanity expressed in the veneration of a Jesus on the cross or a Socrates accepting the cup of death is, as far as it goes, a religiously valid attitude. If that kind of appreciation is the extent of your religiousness, either Jesus or Socrates will do. You will have no need of such things as accounts of the appearance of a risen Lord. There are many persons, some of whom would call themselves Christians, who can read the Gospel accounts and therein identify their own religious sentiments, but they will read no further than the crucifixion, because what lies beyond that is embarrassing. But it is exactly here that the distinctive character of Christian faith begins to emerge. The religious experience of the earliest Christians could not be adequately summed up in terms of Jesus' moral teachings and exemplary life and death. Even pagans of old could accept that. The earliest Christians were experiencing something more, although they were not yet experiencing it very clearly.

The more I read the New Testament record, the more I am persuaded that the early Christian reports of post-Resurrection appearances reflect an entirely new level of reality not experienced prior to the Resurrection. At the same time I am equally persuaded that the early Christians had only a meager and fragmentary apprehension of what it was that was coming to possess them, but that they were being possessed by a newness of life they could not deny.

Surely we must take the apostle Paul seriously when he says, "Now we see as through a glass darkly," or, again to quote the New English Bible, "Now we see only puzzling reflections in a mirror." Indeed, we misread the accounts of the appearances of the risen Lord if we think of them as having all the palpability of tactile character, all the embodiment of our ordinary existence, but we fail to understand Christian faith if we fail to accept the suggestion in these appearances that the ultimate quality of existence is not to be apprehended in our ordinary experiences. What these appearances say to us is that what we are to become, what we move toward, is manifested to us only in vague and fragmentary snatches, but these presentiments of renewal, these phantasmal shadowings of a future condition, these fuzzy outlines portending shapes and circumstances yet to be, these, and not our present circumstances, are the valid definition of our nature and existence. What is difficult for the modern man is to believe that the appearances took place literally as they are reported. But what the Christian cannot deny without losing his Christianity is that these accounts reflect genuine experience with an emerging and new level of life. They are, therefore, not experiences which can be recognized in terms of anything that had gone before, and therefore they left the earliest disciples and us full of perplexity about what it is that is coming—but never in any doubt about the coming of the renewal of life.

All too frequently we read these Gospel passages as if they were reporting the last stages of Jesus' earthly existence. We read of these events as if they were a series of strung-out farewells, a kind of afterglow to the earthly ministry and career of Jesus. When we so interpret these appearances, they are very weak and watery and much less real than the reality of Jesus prior to his crucifixion. But these appearances were not the curtain calls after the drama of redemption had been played out. They are the opening notes of a new time and a new world, with only a fragmentary and suggestive quality—something like an overture to a new drama. The appearances do not restore the earthly Jesus of Nazareth, but they are a revelation of the eternal Christ. They enabled the Apostle Paul to say, "Now is Christ risen from the dead, and becomes the first fruits of them that sleep," although the full harvest lies ahead. The risen Christ is not a concluding episode but the first evidence of a new beginning whose full character remains hidden.

In the writings of C. P. Snow I have found two illustrations that partially illuminate the way in which I believe we must understand these Gospel accounts. In one of Snow's novels, a major character undergoes a personality collapse in which the professional career he had launched comes to nothing and he enters a period that is a sort of personal doldrums. Soon after this apathetic period begins, the man occasionally is roused to carry out some relatively sketchy activities. After a while, a close friend realizes that these occasional activities are the beginning of a new personality structure coming into existence, and the friend remarks that an emergent ego-structure sometimes begins to give evidence of its development many months before it can be identified in any firm or positive way. The accounts of the appearances of the risen Lord are, first and foremost, evidences of something new happening in the world and amongst the disciples, something which they could by no means yet identify, but it began to turn their eyes and concerns toward the future. Here the second suggestion from C. P. Snow applies. In his Godkin Lectures at Harvard University, now published under the title *Science and Government*, Snow distinguishes between what he calls existentialist societies and future-oriented societies. An existentialist society is one which understands itself in terms of its present character and existence; a future-oriented society is one which understands and defines itself in terms of goals which it deeply intends to achieve. There is nothing more clear about the early Christians than the fact that they had passed through experiences which moved them from understanding and defining themselves in terms of their present condition and character. Instead, they began to define themselves in terms of character and qualities yet to be born in them, even though they could not state those characteristics with any kind of precision. Nothing is more characteristic of the faith of the early Christians than its firmness amidst the imprecision of the outcome of faith. This attitude is expressed in the first epistle of John where he says, "Beloved, we are God's children now; it does not appear what we shall be, but we know that when he appears we shall be like him, for we shall see him as he is." The same attitude was expressed in our morning lesson from the first epistle of Peter, "Through the resurrection we have been born anew to a salvation ready to be revealed at the end of the time." From this standpoint we are not to evaluate this world or to estimate ourselves in terms of our present infirm and imperfect state but are to understand the true nature of reality and our own human nature in terms of a holiness yet to be achieved.

In my childhood there was a table grace often sung at church dinners and Sunday school picnics which ran thus:

> Be present at our table, Lord,
> Be here and everywhere adored,
> These mercies bless and grant that we
> May feast in paradise with thee.

During my adolescence and early adulthood this table grace dropped out of use. About a decade ago it came back into use in a modified form. Whoever made the modification thought it was an improvement, and for a while I accepted it as an improvement.

> Be present at our table, Lord,
> Be here and everywhere adored,
> These mercies bless and grant that we
> May feast in fellowship with thee.

Substituting "fellowship" instead of "paradise" undoubtedly freed this little thanksgiving from intellectual embarrassment. Ours is an age which has no idea about where paradise is, and now that space is becoming occupied by us humans we seem to be shouldering the Lord and his heavens out of the skies in order to put our own cities there. But if we do not know where paradise is, we do know what fellowship is. We know also that real fellowship is difficult to achieve and that it is a blessing if we can achieve that much. True friendship is a moral challenge, and to petition that we may feast in fellowship is already to ask a great deal. But the more I used this modified version of the little hymn, the more discontent I became. I became discontent with it as a Christian. Fellowship is still a characteristic within the ordinary human range, and while Christianity appreciates its values, Christianity ultimately talks about newness of life. The result has been a desire to return to the original, even though it means a return to an undefined and fuzzy word: these mercies bless and grant that we may feast in paradise with thee.

There is another way in which we can understand the truly primitive and fragmentary character of the early Christian experience with the risen Lord. It is the recognition that for us the experience of the risen Christ is so much more complete than it ever was for Jesus' earthly followers. That may strike you as a strange statement, but I am convinced that in our day and time we have the advantage of sharing in some of the historic outworkings of the Christian faith. The earliest Christians had only whatever apprehensions they were reporting in terms of those few appearances. They may have been very strong experiences, but they were also fleeting. In the later New Testament times, a strength from the faith could point to a growing company witnessing to the faith, could sense the emerging Church as a continuing Body of Christ, and could speak more and more of his presence. Where the earliest Christians could experience the meaning of Christianity only within a small company, we today are often born into the midst of its love; we have experiences with persons of some holiness of spirit; we have hymns and sermons and ceremony and buildings and art and theologies and creeds and a thousand other supports to our Christian faith of which the earliest generations knew very little.

Edward Scribner Ames, a Hyde Park Minister and university professor of a generation ago, wrote this testimony:

Jesus Christ is actually more alive today than he was before his death. He influences more people, he is better understood, he is more inspiring and more comforting. It is pathetic to hear people repining that they did not live to know him in his physical lifetime, for it only means that they do not know that they have better opportunities to be acquainted with his whole life, and his purposes, and their significance for the world, than the most intimate of his disciples could possibly have had.

The appearances of the risen Lord recorded in the Gospel are in one sense no more than sketches from an artist's notebook, no more than a novelist's jotting down of key episodes for his story. But they were also the way in which the early Christians reported the presence of the risen Lord in their midst. They were reporting a living presence that challenged their unbelief, and whenever you and I behold the wounds given by injustice, the living Christ wrestles with our souls asking that we believe in him. The early Christians were reporting a living presence which turned them from concern about their own welfare and called instead that they take up the shepherding of the flock of God. Wherever you and I confront human need, the living presence wrestles with us to create in us a larger charity. They reported a living presence which sat down with them to eat and drink but it was on behalf of something more than the immediate fellowship of the moment; it was on behalf of paradise.

6

OTHER FAITHS, OTHER LANDS

The Spectator's Perils

By Cecil Northcott
Lutterworth Press, London, England

The text that I would like to offer you this morning
is contained in the Acts of the Apostles in the first chapter,
eleventh verse: "Men of Galilee, why do you stand looking into
heaven?" I stood recently on the so-called Mount of the Ascension—that little bit of a hill which extrudes itself on the Mount
of Olives in Jerusalem. I expect some of you have been there too.
It is nothing much to look at and, of course, there is always the
problem of whether the Ascension really did happen on that spot.
I do not think it matters very much how Jesus was removed
from this earthly scene. We may discuss the methods of his
elevation into heaven. We may probe scientifically into how it
was done, and in the end of the discussion I doubt whether we
shall be very much further on. The issue surely is that the test of
the Christian faith at this point was whether or not it was going
to become simply something to look at, whether it was to be a
religion at which you were going to gaze, whether it was going
to be an experience that you were to be a spectator of, or whether
or not you were really going to be involved in it.

Christianity could so easily have become a company
of men and women who were stargazers. They could have continued the experience of gazing into heaven. Christianity could
have become a company of starry-eyed idealists. A little group of
men and women huddled together there in Jerusalem who would
have tried to remember what he was like, what he said, what he

did. They could have lived on their memories. And it is when Christianity lives on its memories that it is in very real danger of being extinguished. Men of Galilee, why do you stand looking into heaven?

This experience of the Ascension surely foretold the coming experience of Pentecost. To my mind the two great experiences are linked together. You cannot have one without the other. The coming of the Pentecost experience just after this was surely an announcement that in Christ there had entered into the world a new dimension. There had come into the world a new sense and a new purpose. God had intervened into human affairs, and the task of ordinary men and women was not merely to stand gazing at the prospect but to be involved in it.

I would like to look at this experience in three ways this morning—internationally, and in the Church, and for ourselves.

I come from a country which is very much given to spectatoritis. Britain has for many years now been gazing into heaven. Looking at the glorious history of the past, it has been standing on its own Mount of Ascension, expecting that new wonders would descend from the heavens to give it new life and new purpose. After having been away from my own country for a few weeks, I realize that, as you do when you are away from your own particular environment, there are tremendous dangers in being a spectator. To have lost the empire of the New World, the Americas, was certainly a happening of tremendous importance in the life of Britain. To have lost the empire of India was another one. To have lost the empire of the Pacific was another. And to have lost the empire of Africa is the latest of these traumatic experiences which have descended upon the British people. We are open to all the dangers of gazing into heaven, expecting something new and wonderful to happen out of the skies.

I think that the big events which are rescuing Britain from the danger of being a spectator are the re-enlightenment and re-invigoration and renewal of contemporary life in that tiny group of islands in the foggy and misty North Sea. Many great experiences of culture and civilization have come in the past thousand years from those remote offshore islands near the mainland of Europe. For Britain the test of being a great nation now is not the achievement of new geographical empires, but whether or no it is possible that there shall be a new re-invigoration of local life and local purpose. I see it in the building of a new group of universities. The domination of the ancient universities of Oxford and Cambridge, with their boat races, their nice little inhibitions and prohibitions, the pleasantries of belonging to one university or another, is fast fading out. If there is going to be a recovery of culture and civilization, there has got to be a recovery of what it means to be a university. Hoisting the signal that we no longer gaze into heaven expecting the wonders to descend upon us, we work for them, and we dig ourselves in to achieve them.

I see it also in the creation of a whole new range of towns and cities which have not grown up in the "Victorian anyhow," but which have been planned and organized and marshaled from the start. That kind of experience is calling for the young architect, the young musician. It is calling for the young litterateur. It is calling for the new type of journalist. It is calling for the new kind of person who is going to draw new strengths and new wonder from his local life.

We in Britain suffer a very great deal from the fact that we have only one really major and great city. London dominates the island, and it is to resist the domination of a central block in the life of England that the new life in the localities is beginning. I see this also happening in the new industries, in the new techniques, in the new capacity of using the God-given gifts which we have had over the years in new ways.

The Mount of the Ascension must come alive in the local life of the people. If I may say so, the danger of spectatoritis may also be seen in your own country. This constant gazing at the moon, this tremendous eagerness to know about Mars—and Mars, of course, is proving very disappointing. It is very sad that Mars is turning out to be very different from what we expected. It is a nasty, dense sort of place. It has not got any life on it. It is not living up to its reputation. There are no Martians. It looks as if we still have to be content with the planet Earth. It looks as if we still have to be men of God on this planet, and instead of gazing into the heavens, we have more and more to be involved in the life and death and the resurrection of human life on this planet. I wonder whether the total cost of the tremendous machinery which has been erected for the discovery of the wonders of space, whether the cost of all that, if it were put into life on this planet, could not solve many of the problems that we are daily confronted with as ordinary human beings. Men of Galilee, why stand you looking into heaven?

I see this also in the problems of the Christian church. The Christian church is constantly open to the perils of just being a spectator. It is only eleven years now that, on the various campuses of the Chicago area, we had that very remarkable assembly, the Second Assembly of the World Council of Churches. And here over this great area, men and women from every country came for the two-week Assembly to recognize that in Christ Jesus they are all one. I have been going over some of the records of that Assembly recently, and it is amazing to see the hopes and dreams that were enunciated there on the Evanston campus eleven years ago. How very few of those dreams have really come true. If the Christian Gospel is really an urgent Gospel, if the Christian message is really one for men and women of Galilee, then surely we are under the total compulsion of seeing that so many of the resolutions that we passed in these great ecumenical assemblies are really put into action.

We are inclined to think that the authentic experiences of the Christian faith emanate only from the great assemblies of the Christian church. Some of them do, but the test of them always is whether or not we are making them local in their effect. If you want to make religion real, you have to make it local. That was the challenge on the Mount of the Ascension. These men and women had to get off of the top of the hill and get down into the valley of decision, because it was there that the issues of life and death were going to be fought out.

I happen to live in England in the university city of Cambridge, and there are two churches in that city which have existed side by side for centuries. One is a very high Anglo-Catholic church and the other is a Congregational church. They are separated by a passageway that is no wider than the central aisle of this church. But those two churches have rarely been on speaking terms. They have been spectators of one another. They have looked at each other. They have often criticized one another without knowing the truth about each other, and the two great Christian traditions represented in those two churches have marched alongside without meeting. But in the Lenten period of this year, the rector of the Anglo-Catholic church went to see the minister of the Congregational church and suggested to him that it might be a good idea if, on Palm Sunday, the two churches should do something quite dramatic and new. He extended an invitation to the Congregationalists to take part in the rather ritualistic ceremony of the blessings of the palms.

The minister put it to his rather staid puritan Congregational congregation, and they agreed they would go to the other church across the passageway and that they would take part in the blessing of the palms. So with incense reeking around the church, with the palms being held aloft by little boys dressed in all the robes that could be discovered, those two churches celebrated together, in that one church, the event of Christ's entry into Jerusalem. A few days after the ceremony, the rector of the church came to the Congregational church meeting and explained the meaning and the interest of this particular ceremony. I think that experience led those two churches to realize that if they were going to bring all the teachings and all the resolutions of the recent ecumenical assemblies of the churches to the world, they really had to bring it down into life where they are. "Men of Galilee, don't stand looking into heaven."

We are enduring, or going to endure, in England another experience of a similar character in the long-range discussions between Methodists and the Anglican churches. It looks as if the 150-year separation between those two churches is at last going to be bridged. It is going to take a long time to accomplish, but at last those who stand on the Mount of the Ascension and deliver great orations about the wonders of the one united church are getting down to the details of how to do it.

Each of us personally, I think, is open to the sin of being a spectator. One of the most encouraging things, if I may say so, which America is offering to the world at the present time is not the race to the moon, not the discovery of Mars, but the sending out of those young men and women in your Peace Corps, giving a year or two of their young lives to service in all parts of the world. That is the kind of inspiration that we expect to come from this great country, which is now the leader of world affairs. That is the kind of nation-building which can come out of the Christian faith. During this past two thousand years of Christian life, the great missionary movement has been the prime sample of that kind of expansion, the offering of individual dedication. I think that the Peace Corps is offering young men and women in your country the sense of adventure, the sense of life-giving, the sense of being a person, which is surely at the heart of the Christian Gospel. There is a challenge here, I think, for every one of us to be a person in himself, in his own locality. Sometimes I think that you here in America are far too generous with your money. You are far too eager to give your dollars to almost any appeal. You are far too anxious to help. The issue is not whether or not we are really going to involve ourselves in other people's lives but whether we are really going to give ourselves to a great cause and not produce the easy alibi of money. Money is only a symbol of personality, but the issue of this text, I think, lies not with money, not with alibis; it lies with each of us, giving himself where he is, and recognizing that merely to be a spectator of life is to continue gazing into heaven. "Ye men and women of Galilee, why stand gazing?"

You Are the Letter of Christ

Masao Takenaka
Doshisha University, Kyoto, Japan

      I would like for a few moments to reflect with you upon the passages from II Corinthians which we heard this morning. This is a letter addressed to a small Christian congregation in the vast non-Christian world. The Church is a younger church without a long-established tradition. Most of the members are not those who were born into this religious community. On the contrary, they came to take part in the new community through their conversion, a turning of the mind from the old way to a new life which they received in Jesus Christ. In fact, most of them were just baptized, but they became Christian with decisive commitment and irreplaceable joy and hope.

      This is a very important factor for us to remember. We Asian Christians are also living in a minority situation. In Japan, the Christian community, including Orthodox, Roman Catholics, and Protestants, is less than one per cent of the total population.

      In the so-called Western countries where Christianity takes a majority position, there is a temptation for men and women to become Christians too easily. When a baby is born, he receives baptism as if receiving a vaccination. In this technological age, automation is going on even in the process of becoming Christian. You accept the Christian religion because this nation traditionally was founded on Christian principles. You go to a church because others in the community go to that church.

215

But in Asia, the reasons are reversed. Christians attend church not because of the external social and cultural influences, but in spite of the oppositions, indifference, or even the persecution of the society about them. Men and women commit themselves to accept the truth in love revealed in the drama of redemption in Jesus Christ. Something happens within them.

But we must not idealize the so-called younger churches. We must guard against the myth of younger churches, a tendency to paint the picture of the younger churches in a too-beautiful or too-idealistic way. In this sense, we need to demythologize the younger churches. A younger church is also a human community. It is a place of sinners among sinners. It is an earthly vessel, yet the divine light permeates it constantly.

Look at the church in Corinth. First of all it consisted of a rather simple and ordinary group of working people and their families. According to Acts 18, when Paul went to Corinth, "he found a couple of displaced Jews called Aquila and his wife Priscilla. Because he was of the same trade, tent-making, he stayed with them and they worked together."

We are glad to note that the Christian community was founded among the ordinary working people in Corinth. They were shopkeepers, tent-makers, handicraftsmen, housewives and slaves, simple, poor, and ordinary people. In today's terms, they were grocery store men, repairmen, gas station attendants, working wives, and cleaning ladies. As the Apostle writes, "Not many of them were wise according to worldly standards, not many were powerful, not many were of noble birth, but God chooses what is weak in the world to shame the strong. God chooses what is low and despised in the world to bring to nothing things that are" (I Cor. 1:26–28).

This has a dual meaning to the contemporary situation. First, we have confidence and joy to be the Christian community, but it does not come out of the world, nor can we claim it as being rooted in ourselves. Our confidence and joy is rooted in him who took the suffering and burdens of the world and rose from the dead as a first fruit of the new humanity. This concept of the first fruit is an illuminating concept for us. Particularly for those of us living in Asia.

Secondly, this community of Christians exists in a particular place as a representative figure and image of the Christ. Even today, we still have to overcome the fact that we are in a minority situation. In spite of the numbers, the first fruits are the symbols and representatives in the particular place where they are, where they work, where they travel, where they spend their leisure time, in their homes, university, store, political office, and women's clubs.

For this context Paul writes that you are a letter from Christ. He does not say you are the person to carry a letter of Christ written on a piece of paper as a certificate for good life in heaven. Neither is he saying that you are the person to speak about the letter of Christ with a theological explanation and exegesis. He is saying you are yourselves a letter from Christ, not written with ink but with the Spirit of the living God—not on tablets of stone, but on tablets of human hearts. This means that your heart and body, your total existence, is a living and visible letter from Christ, to be known and read by all men.

Here is a voice of the Asian church which reflected the same concern when they met together at Kuala Lumpur for the Inaugural Assembly of the East Asian Christian Conference. It says, "Each congregation must know it is put into the world by the Lord as his representative, and that it must therefore be chiefly concerned not with itself, but with the world, concerned to send its members out as witnesses and to invite all men into the family of God. Its minister should be one who is seeking to train every member for his ministry in the world." It must not be said of the new churches that they are too small to be missionaries, but they must ask whether they are missionary-minded enough to be strong.

Today in this highly complex, industrial and technological society in which we live, the pattern of the communication of the Christian faith must be re-examined. The man in the street today is not interested in hearing a one-sided monologue. He is sick and tired of self-exalted lip service and neat and nice words of propaganda. Yet he is hungry for a real letter, not one written on paper with ink, but one written by the Spirit on tablets of human hearts. He is searching to meet a man who lives with him in the sharing of the ordinary burdens of life in his daily work but yet someone who does not lose an outlook of humanity or hope.

In each period of history when Christianity made a distinctive contribution, we find there was a distinctive Christian style of life. A style of martyr contending against the persecution of the Roman Empire was distinctive in the age of the early Church. There was a style of saintly, holy living in the Middle Ages. In the sixteenth century there came a new style of life that was carried out by the Reformers.

During the eighteenth and nineteenth centuries, a distinctive Christian style of living may also be found. This may be called a puritanistic or pietistic style of living and is becoming an out-of-date, worn-out tradition. Today we must again ask ourselves, What is the Christian style of living in the world?

In the Scripture passages of this morning we heard rather illuminating phrases which are somehow inspiring as well as astonishing. They are even irritating when we note that they were written to a handful of simple, ordinary people in the church at Corinth. I am referring to such words that characterize their presence, their involvement in the world as if we are the aroma of Christ. Through us Christ spreads the fragrance of the knowledge of him everywhere . . ." (II Cor. 2:14–15), "the great splendor and freedom in spirit" (II Cor. 3:8), and above all, their lives "being changed into his likeness from one degree of glory to another" (II Cor. 3:18).

In spite of the fact that they were a small, poor, suffering Christian community that consisted of ordinary working men and women, they encountered one decisive event—God lifted up the veil and the mystery of truth was revealed in Christ. It was in a real and concrete event in history that God became real man in order that man might become a real man.

One of the struggling yet most challenging frontiers of missions of the Church in Japan is among working people in the industrial society. The Kyodan, the United Church of Christ in Japan, organized in 1951 a committee called the National Committee on Occupational Evangelism. In each of fourteen presbyteries there is a corresponding committee. They keep their eyes open to the people in the industrial society in order to fulfill the Christian responsibility in that urgent field of the modern society.

One of the most encouraging signs in this field is the works of a writer called Rinzo Shiina, one of the popular novelists of contemporary Japan. Through his unique and lucid literary style, he presents vividly the ordinary problems of ordinary Japanese working people. One of the reasons his novels are so widely read among the contemporary Japanese is that he writes them from his own concrete experience, namely, out of his direct encounter with the problems of life in the industrial society as an ordinary worker. In this sense we may call his novels the first Christian existential novels of the Japanese industrial society.

It is not easy to interpret Shiina's writing, since the non-religious language and pictures in his novels can be interpreted in different ways. However, his personal background can help us to understand what he tries to express. He was born in Himeji, in the western part of Japan, in 1911. He had to quit school at 15 in the middle of his secondary education owing to poverty and a divorce in his family. First he worked in a restaurant as a dishwasher. Then he became a railroad worker and joined a labor union. He was a sincere man with a single-hearted devotion to work for the welfare and rights of the working people. Partly because of force applied by the leaders of the movement, he became a member of the Communist Party.

In 1931, he was captured by the police and put into prison, and there was subject to torture. This did not change his mind; so he received a four-year sentence. One time, in cold weather, several degrees below the freezing point, he was put naked in a large room and beaten with a bamboo stick. A policeman also threw buckets of cold water over his head. Looking back on the experience, he writes, "I felt the nearness of my death, not as an idea but in actuality. Not the death of other men but my own death." He felt a deep frustration because he recognized that his friends had betrayed him. He was alone in prison and began to reflect upon himself honestly. He became more and more self-critical. What was in his mind was not the faces of

comrades of the Communist Party or even the faces of his close
family circle; he only thought of himself, under the fear of death
and wanting to live.

He realistically saw the finiteness and egocentric
reality of man. Ever since, he has searched for a source of power to
overcome death and despair of man. His search carried him from
the traditional pattern of thinking through Nietzsche, Dostoevski, and finally he found hope in Jesus Christ.

One of the characteristics of the Japanese novel is that
there is a constant tone of tragedy. There is a kind of deterministic
acceptance of one's fate with an attitude of resignation. It is an
almost nihilistic picture without an outlook of hope. As a result,
quite often a central figure commits suicide or loses his senses.
But in Shiina's novel there is an image of man which is distinctively different. His characters live an ordinary gray life of routine
drudgery among illicit human relations and under the pressure
of economic necessity, and they are confronted with a rigid,
feudalistic kind of life. They work and live; they smoke and drink,
and they make mistakes. In this sense they are not different from
characters of other novels.

But in one thing they are distinctively different, for
somehow they do not lose an outlook of hope. The reader tends
to anticipate when they will commit suicide or give up by resign-
ing themselves to the tragedy of human existence, but they smile
in the midst of tribulation and struggle in the world. It is a
strange smile which does not come from themselves. They know
well that they cannot absolutize the earthly power and strength,
either the power of economic wealth or the power of the political
situation. For them, even death is not final. Theirs is a laughter
or humor which does not depend upon themselves or any human
ability or strength. It is a humor given to a man who sees a
peculiar contrast within himself and the world. It is a kind of
realized freedom given to a forgiven sinner by grace.

To be a Christian means to be a man rooted in Christ,
who is the first fruits of the new humanity. It means accepting
Christ by turning one's whole existence. The Christian is also
called the first fruits as a representative figure for the great harvest
to be. In this sense he stands in the secular world, either in the

factory or office, either in the home or women's club, as a first fruits of the new humanity. He radiates the fragrance of humanity by constantly seeking to live between men with a spirit of solidarity without losing an outlook of hope and freedom.

So let us turn to the Lord. As the Scripture says, "the veil is removed." Now the Lord is the Spirit and where the Spirit of the Lord is, there is freedom. And we all, with unveiled faces, beholding the glory of the Lord, are being changed into his likeness from one degree of glory to another, for this comes from the Lord who is the Spirit (II Cor. 3:17).

In Christ the Twain Shall Meet

By Otto Meinardus
American University, Cairo, Egypt

From the Prophecy of Hosea: "Out of Egypt have I called my Son."

He who travels in the Valley of the Nile visiting the small and overcrowded mud-brick villages cannot help noticing those many sites which commemorate the flight of the holy family into Egypt. Indeed, the belief that our Savior was called out of the land of the pharaohs is as vital to the Coptic Christians of Egypt as the landing of the Pilgrims on the shores of New England might be to the American Christians. In spite of the fact that Egypt is one of the first Christian countries, our knowledge of the Nile Valley Christians is blurred by our ignorance and the accumulated prejudices of the past 1,500 years.

In these days, the Christian world in both the Orient and the Occident is literally swamped with news and reports of the Ecumenical Council held under the auspices of the See of Rome, and the ideas and the concepts of ecumenicity have become widely popularized. Fifty years ago, only a few theologians understood what was meant by ecumenicity. Today, practically everybody has some notion about its meaning and significance.

For the Latin Christian, ecumenicity means, among other things, the theological and ecclesiological encounter of the Church of Rome with the non-Roman churches throughout the world. For most Protestants, ecumenicity has meant either a striving toward better relations, or co-operation, or even merger of Protestant denominations. Yet most of us have thought of ecumenicity in terms of some sort of pan-Protestantism, in which Baptists and Methodists, Lutherans and Episcopalians might engage in common projects, be it on the local, national, or international level.

Ever since New Delhi, however, a new dimension has been added to our ecumenical thinking. Several millions of Orthodox Christians, of whom we had just a vague knowledge, entered the ecumenical dialogue, and no longer can we uphold the pan-Protestant image in our ecumenical thinking.

For the first time in 1,600 years, Orient and Occident are drawn together in theological conversation and debate. For the first time since the Reformation, we find Methodist ministers encountering Antiochene archimandrites, we see Presbyterian scholars engage in serious conversation with the hermits of the Egyptian deserts.

Indeed, a new era has emerged—an era in which potentially East and West can meet in Jesus Christ, our common Lord and Savior. Thus, whatever I am going to say should help us as Occidental or Western Christians to understand this new dimension into which our Savior Christ has brought us. For remember, he whose body is divided by theological and non-theological factors prayed that all may be one.

In the past, we may have had our difficulties in appreciating the traditions and religious expressions of our various Protestant brethren. Yet, the common heritage of the Reformation provided us with sufficient understanding to engage in fruitful conversation. The more severe, and at the same time the more tragic, divisions of the Body of Christ, however, occurred at a time when the Orient was alienated from the Occident.

Occidental Christianity, with its pragmatic and activistic attitudes, its striving for quantitative success, its pragmatic social and philosophical theology, may find it difficult to appreciate the theological values of the Orient. In addition to the real intellectual difficulties of seeing in hermits and anchorites a practical application of the evangelic precept to abandon all things and to follow Christ, there exists in the Occident and the

Orient an inexcusable ignorance of their respective traditions, theologians, and saints. Just as the desert fathers are unaware of the contributions of such theologians as St. Thomas Aquinas, Luther, Calvin, Barth, or Tillich; Methodists, Presbyterians, and Episcopalians have little comprehension of the spiritual encounters of St. Paphnutius or the charismatic works of the blessed Abraham of the Fayum. In spite of the fact that God called his son out of Egypt, we share little knowledge of the Christians in Egypt or any other part of the Orient. Since their forms of worship, their witness, yes, their theology appear to us so strange, so utterly alien, we either shrug our shoulders or are even apt to cover our ignorance with Occidental smugness and subtle ridicule.

A good illustration of our misunderstanding is provided by the widespread disappointment of Occidental pilgrims or tourists to the holy city of Jerusalem. Expecting to see the holy sites preserved in their natural beauty and simplicity, many Protestants have expressed their utter disgust that almost every sacred site is covered and obliterated by a church, an altar, or an oratory. Well, the Oriental Christians, who had made their pilgrimages to Jerusalem ever since the fourth century went to the holy places to worship and to pray. They never thought of Jerusalem or Bethlehem in terms of a site, the original identity of which was to be preserved. They never thought of it as a natural museum through which one may pass in quiet devotion. On the contrary, those who worship through the celebration of the divine liturgy would naturally build chapels over those sites which commemorate the agony and passion of our Savior. Thus many Protestant Christians have the feeling of being left out, not realizing their unusual favorable position which enables the Protestant to worship him in spirit and in truth. Thus, we should find it not difficult to meet the Christ, no matter whether the shrine happens to be Armenian, Latin, Greek, or Ethiopian. Instead of being disappointed by the manner in which the Oriental Christians worship, we might well practice that humility by which we may gain insight into that spirituality of which the Occident knows so little.

For centuries, the Occident has exposed itself to the Orient. Politically, economically, and religiously, the West has penetrated into the Orient. Religiously speaking, we have brought our Western ideas to bear upon the people of the Orient. Ever since the fourteenth century, Franciscan friars have spread Occidental theological thinking among Arabs, Copts, and Ethiopians. Since the nineteenth century, Protestants of the various shades and denominations have entered the race in converting the Orient either to a seventeenth-century Calvinism or a eighteenth-century puritanical pietism. In our days, however, those who once were the objects of our missionary zeal have become our brothers and partners with whom we sit as equals at conference tables. The question which I pose is whether in this century our growth in grace and understanding can mature without the light from the East, the very Orient which gave us Moses, Elijah, yes, which gave us the Christ—the very Orient that produced the noble company of martyrs and confessors, doctors and theologians.

To be sure, it was not until I had encountered the fathers of the desert, the hermits and anchorites of the wide and open spaces, miles removed from the cultivated land, that I became aware of this new dimension which confronts our ecumenical conversation. Indeed, the time is at hand, when we, who have one foot in the Orient and the other in the Occident, must bear witness to the Western churches of the heritage of the Orient.

Out of Egypt, the Lord had called his son, and thus the land was blessed by the holy family when, after being advised by the angel, they fled first to the Delta of the Nile and from there proceeded southward along the Nile Valley. Egyptian Jews participated in the Pentecostal celebrations in Jerusalem. There they were converted by the powerful preaching of St. Peter and subsequently returned to their homes in Alexandria or to the Babylon on the Nile. It was St. Mark the Evangelist who is credited with organizing these Christian pockets into a Church, and to this very day, the head of the Church, the Pope of Alexandria is referred to as the one-hundred sixteenth successor of the See of St. Mark—a Church that has suffered martyrdom, ostracism, and persecution ever since its birth; a Church which ever since the fifth century has lived in complete isolation from the Byzantine East and the Latin West; a Church that has provided World Christianity with the institution of monasticism, that culture bearing and maintaining agent of the Middle Ages; a Church that has supplied the World Church with the first great theological pioneers at the Catechetical School of Alexandria. This church is made up of a group of Christians whose life, worship, and theology we have great difficulty to understand. Yet, if Christ speaks through the ecumenical movement, then, he, being an Oriental, also speaks to us through the ancient Oriental church.

Between Cairo and Alexandria there is the famous Desert of Scetis, which in the fifth and sixth centuries was occupied by literally thousands of hermits and anchorites. Today, only four desert monasteries remind the pilgrim of this distinguished Christian battleground where the fathers of the desert fought temptations and desires. One of these monasteries is dedicated to St. Bishoi, a famous hermit of the fourth century. While observing the solitary life, St. Bishoi had several visions of the Lord Jesus Christ. Some monks, who had heard about the visions of their abbot, approached him with the request to lead them to the Christ. A few days later, St. Bishoi instructed his monks to proceed to a certain place in the desert where the Christ would await them. As they passed on their way, they saw an old and feeble man asking to be taken along by the monks, but the monks, anxious to meet the Christ, ignored the pleading old man. In the last group of the monks was St. Bishoi, and when he saw the old man, he had compassion on him and carried him along to his destination. After having arrived at the place where they were to meet the Christ, St. Bishoi straightened his back, and the stranger disappeared. The Christ whom the monks were seeking sat at the roadside, waiting to be helped. In their haste for the Christ, they had forgotten to be Christians.

We have gone into the world to proclaim the Gospel of our Savior; we have passed the Orient on our way to convert the Hindus and the Sikhs, the Buddhists and the Moslems; we have passed by the Oriental churches whether in Syria or in Egypt; we have been partners of the unfortunate alienation of the Orient from the Occident.

May the Lord God, who ministered to the people of the Orient and sent his apostles to the people of the Occident, grant to this generation the apostolic wisdom and insight into the mystery of our common faith in Jesus Christ.

DATE DUE